DEATH ON KATAHDIN

DEATH ON KATAHDIN

And Other Misadventures in
Maine's Baxter State Park

RANDI MINETOR

Camden, Maine

Down East Books

An imprint of The Rowman & Littlefield Publishing Group, Inc.
4501 Forbes Blvd., Ste. 200
Lanham, MD 20706
www.rowman.com

Distributed by NATIONAL BOOK NETWORK

British Library Cataloguing in Publication Information available

Library of Congress Cataloging-in-Publication Data available

ISBN 978-1-60893-417-1 (paperback)
ISBN 978-1-60893-418-8 (e-book)

♾™ The paper used in this publication meets the minimum requirements of American National Standard for Information Sciences—Permanence of Paper for Printed Library Materials, ANSI/NISO Z39.48-1992.

Printed in the United States of America

I dedicate this book to all the archivists, historians, and reference and local history librarians who bring to their work a boundless enthusiasm for the scavenger hunt that is historical research. You have my utmost respect and gratitude for your help in making my work possible.

CONTENTS

ACKNOWLEDGMENTS

What a pleasure it is to write about the Maine north woods, especially because I had an unusually generous amount of assistance while researching the stories in this book.

First, the staff at Baxter State Park pointed me in a number of useful directions to find documents and media coverage, helping me fill in the details about incidents that took place decades before they became employees of the park.

Local history and special collections librarian Betsy Paradis at the Bangor Public Library went out of her way to find bits of information that would not have surfaced without her knowledge of local history records. Trudy Wyman, curator of the Millinocket Historical Society, did her best to search newspapers to help me piece together the facts about several deaths in the park, which gave me a better understanding of the limits of information available in Millinocket. In the same vein, the volunteers who now run the Millinocket Public Library gave me access to physical files of fragile newspapers dating back to 1940, and the opportunity to determine that I had all the available information (scant as some of it was) helped bring the project to a satisfying conclusion.

Others who assisted with my research include Carl Langsenkamp, vice president of global public relations at Xerox Corporation, as well as Xerox archives manager Ray Brewer; and the venerable Peter Noddin, administrator of the Maine Wreck Chasers website and database, who helped me track down the details of the 1956 plane crash north of the Brothers Mountains. I thank all of these historians, as well as Craig Fuller of Aviation Archaeological Investigation and Research (AAIR) in Phoenix, Arizona, for pulling the file on the 1944 plane crash on Fort Mountain and sending me all seventy-eight pages of it.

I am especially grateful to Carol Newlin, survivor of the 1968 lightning strike in Chimney Pond Campground, and Charlie Jackson, who helped rescue her, for their willingness to talk with me about their experiences. Likewise, I thank Martha Mott Reynolds, her brother, Greg Mott, and her husband, Mike Reynolds, for so willingly sharing their family's experience in the park in July 1965. I am equally indebted to Steve Tetreault, former Baxter State Park ranger, for his vivid account of fall victim Derek Quiet's recovery mission, both by phone and in his own book. I did not speak directly to Game Warden Eric Wight, but his book proved invaluable as well in filling in the gaps left by scant media coverage and pre-computer recordkeeping.

The folks at Globe Pequot Press always turn out a terrific book, so it continues to be my pleasure to work with them for the twelfth consecutive year. My editor, Michael Steere of Down East Books, and the crew including assistant editor Sarah Parke, production editor Ellen Urban, layout artist Jason Rock, copy editor Jessie Shiers, and proofreader Lauren Szalkiewicz, have all done their usual excellent job in bringing this book to fruition. And I can't say this enough: My agent, Regina Ryan, got me through the door to become a writer on this series of "Death" books, so I thank her once again for keeping an ear to the ground and making the proper connections on my behalf.

Finally, to the friends and family who support all of my writing endeavors: Ken Horowitz and Rose-Anne Moore, Martin Winer, Bruce Barton, Martha and Peter Schermerhorn, Paula and Rich Landis, Ruth Watson and John King, Cindy Blair, Bil Walters and Christine Tattersall, and my adorable husband, Nic Minetor, who has endured often-ghastly dinner-table descriptions of every unfortunate soul in four "Death" books to date . . . I could not do what I do without your encouragement, your indulgence, and your love. Thank you all for being such an important part of my life.

INTRODUCTION:
DEFYING PAMOLA

"Man is born to die, his work is short-lived.
Buildings crumble, monuments decay, wealth vanishes.
But Katahdin in all its glory forever shall remain
the mountain of the people of Maine."
PERCIVAL P. BAXTER, MAINE GOVERNOR 1921–1924

It began as a passion project by an enlightened man with the means to make it happen, and grew to become the crown jewel of a state also rich with ocean beaches, fjord-like bays and sounds, and high granite cliffs. Baxter State Park, named for the man who conceived it, preserves the deep woods and high peaks of northern Maine and now hosts upwards of 60,000 visitors in the summer months alone, including many Maine residents who return over and over to summit one more mountain, fish in one more pond, or hike a different trail to the top of Mount Katahdin.

Percival P. Baxter loved the woods and kettle ponds of northern Maine, so when he had the means and the opportunity, he purchased Katahdin—yes, he bought a mountain—and donated it to the state of Maine, on the condition that it be preserved as wild land forever. This first gift established the method for creating a park, so Baxter kept buying land adjacent to his original purchase. Landowners in the area saw the value in his plan and donated their own land, until the park reached its current size of 209,644 acres, or more than 320 square miles. Today most of the park serves as a wildlife sanctuary, while just under 30,000 acres are managed for sustainable scientific forestry, and more than 52,000 acres are open for hunting and trapping (except for moose, which are protected).

At 5,267 feet, Katahdin is the tallest mountain in Maine—and while its size may seem less than impressive to those who frequent the much younger and higher Rocky Mountains, Katahdin towers mightily over the park's other forty-plus peaks, its summit often encircled with clouds. Its rugged trails, ice-filled gullies in winter, and changeable weather patterns make Katahdin the most challenging climb in the state—and tens of thousands of visitors rise to this challenge year-round, returning without mishap to tell the tale.

Baxter Peak stands as the topmost of the mountain's multiple pinnacles, serving double duty as the terminus of the 2,189.2-mile Appalachian National Scenic Trail. Very slightly lower but even more challenging to reach, Pamola Peak forms the end of the Knife Edge, one of the Northeast's most legendary and precarious stretches of trail. At about a mile long and a mere three feet wide in spots, with granite ledges and boulders sloping downward for more than 1,000 feet on either side, Knife Edge stymies many who consider the option of crossing it. Many hikers, however, delight in the spectacular views of the park on either side, and in the sense that a free fall over serrated rocks could be just a misstep away.

It's almost imperative that such a trail have its own folklore, and the mountain obliges us with the story of Pamola, the bird spirit that the indigenous Abenaki people believed caused winter storms. The volatile spirit lived at the peak, according to legend, and anyone who dared to approach the summit via the Knife Edge, Helon Taylor, or Dudley trails (both named much later) might be subjected to high winds, blinding snow, and paralyzing cold. With modern weather forecasting, it's easier today to tell when Pamola may be fuming atop the mountain, and to plan a hike for a day when the spirit's mood improves.

Which, of course, brings us to the topic of this book. *Death on Katahdin* is obviously not a book about wonderful climbing experiences or pleasant camping trips. This is a book about people who arrived at Baxter State Park expecting to have the time of their lives, and whose visits ended in death.

It's a strange assignment indeed, and a particularly knotty one, as the book's title gives away the ending to every story contained within. I retell these episodes not to frighten you away from the park, but to urge you to take the proper precautions—many of which are detailed in the epilogue of this book—to be sure that your adventure in the park ends as safely as it began.

Since the park recorded its first known loss of life in 1933, sixty-four victims have fallen prey to the challenges of this protected section of the north country. Let me say first that *not one* of these incidents involved an Appalachian Trail (AT) hiker. By the time AT hikers reach Katahdin, they are so seasoned and have climbed so many mountains—including much higher peaks, like Mount Washington in New Hampshire (6,289 feet) and Clingman's Dome in Great Smoky Mountains National Park (6,644 feet)—that finishing the AT here is a comparatively simple task. AT hikers take Baxter State Park's Hunt Trail to the top of this mountain, and the 5.2-mile trail, even with its rock-scrambling Gateway section that requires rebar handholds, serves as a moderate day-hike, requiring only a light day pack instead of the thirty to forty pounds of gear through-hikers routinely carry here from Springer Mountain, Georgia.

Seventeen of the deaths in the park were the result of heart attacks or other medical issues, which I have chosen not to detail in this book. (You will find their names, however, in the chronological list of deaths in the appendix at the end of this volume.) The park issued its own search-and-rescue research report in 2015, detailing activity from 1992 to 2014, and it notes, "Many visitors to Baxter State Park, home of Maine's highest peak, Mt. Katahdin, aspire to summit the mountain and often underestimate the physical conditioning and supplies necessary for navigating the rugged terrain." Heart-attack victims account for barely 1 percent of the search-and-rescue operations that take place in the park—the vast majority are for foot, ankle, or leg injuries—but people who don't realize how difficult the climb will be may require evacuation, either with their hearts intact or without.

Mishaps on Katahdin account for twenty-four of the deaths, including a number of the medical ones, but other areas of the park have seen their share of deadly accidents as well. Nine people died in plane crashes in the park's northernmost mountains, three perished from lightning strikes, and seven drowned. (Two committed suicide, but I have chosen to give them their privacy, so they only appear in the list at the end of the book.)

The people who have the dubious honor of being featured in this book did not, for the most part, take unnecessary chances or play fast and loose with their own lives. In each case, one mistake—a misplaced footfall, a missed weather forecast, or a momentary lapse in judgment—led to a disastrous outcome. In some of these cases, nothing at all could have been done to avoid the situation; sometimes the course nature takes can be deadly for those who have the misfortune to be in its way. Sheer bad luck comes when we least expect it, not on any schedule we may attempt to follow, and those in the path of a giant boulder, a bolt of lightning, or a wall of sliding snow have no opportunity to dodge their fate.

I know that many readers of books in what is known as "the *Death* series" enjoy a little quiet *schadenfreude* that they themselves came home safely, while others did not. Let me say that I do not write these books (including my three earlier volumes, *Death in Glacier National Park*, *Death in Zion National Park*, and *Death on Mount Washington*) to ridicule the actions that resulted in disastrous ends to vacations or bucket-list trips. Instead, I hope that these stories serve as cautionary tales that make readers think twice about the way they approach their own outdoor adventures—and that my readers all take the necessary precautions to stay safe.

In researching these stories, I have plumbed newspaper archives, state park records, historical accounts, books, Library of

Congress photographs, YouTube videos, personal interviews, and other resources to bring you the facts in as journalistic a manner as possible. My goal is to provide you with the information you need to draw your own conclusions about what these people should or should not have done before a final step led them to a bad end. If this book helps you avoid making the same fatal mistake, then I have accomplished my goal.

As thorough as I have sought to be, however, some details never came to light. If you find as you read this that there's something I missed, or that you have information that did not surface for me, I invite you to contact me directly at author@minetor.com. I will add the information to the book's second edition sometime in the future.

Finally, please rest assured that your visit to Baxter State Park will not be dangerous if you proceed with caution, carry what you need for any situation, and stay aware of your surroundings. Less than one person annually loses his or her life in the park, because the risk is only as great as a hiker's lack of preparedness or willingness to recognize when it's time to turn back. I urge you to visit this remarkable place, enjoy the north woods to the fullest, and give Katahdin the respect it commands. Don't let someone else's errors deter you from seeing this magnificent park and exploring it on your own.

Just be careful out there.

CHAPTER 1

The Ten Longest Days:
The Search for the Mott Brothers

MARTHA MOTT REYNOLDS AND HER HUSBAND, MIKE, TURNED the pages of a scrapbook Martha's father, George Mott, had made for her many years ago. "Every summer, from my earliest memories, we went camping because it was a nice, cheap way to spend time away from home," she said. "We'd go someplace where there was swimming and hiking, a pool, a stream, a lake. There were always streams that we could hop rocks across—rock-hopping was one of my favorite things, along with picking up rocks along the edges and finding salamanders. Red efts were the best."

In her home near Brockport, New York, she found the photos she was looking for: pictures of her older brother, Robbie, and Timmy, her youngest brother, in the spring of 1965. Robbie, a slight boy not more than five feet tall, looked more like a child of ten or eleven than a near-adult of seventeen. He and three-year-old Timmy were inseparable, holding hands as they wandered through campgrounds, chased small animals, and gathered wood—branches of spruce and birch that were "dead and down," Martha said, reciting the universal park rule for using wood from the forest for campfires.

More than fifty years since the incident that changed her family's lives forever, she was willing to fill in the details of a story that became national news, one that families across the country followed for ten long days in July 1965.

Martha's father, George Mott, certainly had earned a pleasant vacation with his family. An engineer and inventor, he had completed his PhD in physics at the University of Rochester a few years before, and Chester Carlson, head of a start-up company called Haloid Xerox, Inc., had scooped him up to work with five other scientists on a new dry-writing process Carlson called "xerography." Mott provided his expertise and problem-solving abilities to the team that developed the Xerox 914, the first automatic, plain-paper photocopier, which transferred images from one sheet of paper to another using static electricity. By 1961, the company dropped Haloid from its name and became Xerox Corporation.

In the summer of 1965, Mott took his family—his wife, Ruth, and four children, including Robbie, fifteen-year-old Martha, Greg, who was eleven, and Timothy, as well as Martha's friend Bonnie Grant—to Baxter State Park. The happy group set up camp in their trailer in Roaring Brook Campground, where their children discovered places to hike, splash in shallow ponds, observe wildlife, and run and play in the crisp mountain air.

The Motts taught their children the skills they needed to be comfortable and safe in wilderness areas. "In the early days, we had a great, huge, heavy canvas tent, and a large tarp that attached to it," Martha said. "Then we started camping with a trailer—with four kids, all the luggage needed a place to go, and we needed somewhere easier to sleep. So this was the first trip with the trailer." She smiled as she added, "Dad had a harmonica he was very good at. There was always music around the campfire."

Thursday, July 29, dawned promisingly pleasant. George, Ruth, and Greg left Martha and Bonnie in charge of Robbie and Timmy and set off on a hike to the summit of Mount Katahdin at 5,267 feet, the first time the Mott parents had left some of the family behind while they made a major trek. Their route would take them on a tour of the mountain's summits across the Knife Edge, the slim, serrated top edge trail from Baxter Peak to Pamola Peak, and on to Chimney Pond Campground. If the route proved longer than anticipated and they were still on the trail into the evening, they would stay the night at Chimney Pond and return on the Chimney Pond Trail to Roaring Brook on Friday.

While Robbie was the oldest child, he had a developmental disability—what the 1960s press indelicately labeled as "mentally retarded"—that limited his emotional growth to that of a much younger child. His family was also vigilant to another health issue, however: Robbie had type 1 diabetes, requiring close monitoring and insulin injections twice daily.

Things went swimmingly at Roaring Brook on Thursday. Martha and Bonnie saw the boys periodically during the afternoon as Robbie and Timmy walked in circles around the whole campground, watching wildlife, collecting wood, and visiting briefly with other families camped there. "It was absolutely normal for the two of them to go off together hand in hand, and in this particular campground it was a circle," said Martha. "We'd watch them go by—we'd sit outside and watch what was happening, or we'd go into the trailer, but at least one of us was always at the campsite. The two of us girls should have been able to make sure everything was normal."

The boys reappeared every fifteen to twenty minutes, so it was easy to keep tabs on them as they circled the campground. But on one trip, they did not emerge after the usual interval. Martha and Bonnie began to wonder what had become of the two boys.

"We watched and watched, and they didn't come back around, and we determined that they weren't coming back," Martha said. "We walked around to other campsites and we talked to people."

Several campers noted that they had observed the boys along the camp road, but not in the last hour or so. By 6 p.m., Martha went to the ranger station near the campsite and notified the camp ranger, Wilbur Smith, that she could not find the boys. Smith conducted a limited search and then put the word out to the Maine Game Warden Service, and Warden Eric Wight responded. "Upon our arrival, Ranger Rodney Sargent and I discovered that the two brothers . . . had not been seen since afternoon," Wight wrote in his book, *Life and Death in the North Woods: The Story of the Maine Game Warden Service.* "We spent the night going up and down along the banks of Roaring Brook, looking for clues. Earlier in the day, the boys had been at Sandy Stream Pond not far from the campsite, so we looked in that area also."

Meanwhile, word went out throughout the park that two children were lost in the woods. George, Ruth, and Greg Mott had arrived at Chimney Pond Campground and were about to make camp for the night, when the ranger's radio crackled to life.

Greg Mott, speaking recently from his home in St. Paul, Minnesota, remembers that moment. "Mom and Dad heard the noise on the radio about boys being lost," he said. "They asked, 'What boys are those?' When they heard it was Robbie and Timmy, they made the decision to go down, and gosh, the rangers there warned us that it would be getting dark, and hard to find the trail. They couldn't send someone with us because they didn't have enough people in order to do that."

Needless to say, no parents could sit and wait until morning knowing that their children were lost in the park. George, Ruth, and Greg repacked their belongings in the gathering dusk and started down the Chimney Pond Trail—a rugged, three-and-a-half-mile route loaded with jagged rocks, uneven surfaces, and awkward scrambles. The trail challenges hikers in broad daylight; at night, its difficulty rises to treacherous levels.

"We had flashlights, and sure enough, it was tricky," said Greg. "There were several times when Mom and I would stay in one place while Dad explored the trail down what might have been a wash. There were times when they were both away and I was standing there waiting, and they were out with their flashlights, which were running low."

As they approached the bottom of the long downhill route, they met a ranger making his way up the trail to meet them with flashlights. "He escorted us the rest of the way," said Greg. When they arrived at Roaring Brook Campground, other campers reported that they had seen two boys fitting the Mott brothers' description playing in a corner of Roaring Brook Camp as late as 7 p.m. "This was about an hour and a half after the other girls in our party had reported the boys as missing to the camp ranger," George Mott told a reporter from his hometown Rochester paper, the *Democrat & Chronicle*, the following day.

Both boys were dressed in sweaters, and Timothy wore jeans while Robbie wore a pair of shorts, comfortable clothing for the day's average temperature of sixty-two degrees, but less than required to resist the chill that arrived after sunset. The night's temperature dropped to forty-six degrees, low enough to create a dangerous situation for a three-year-old too young to have wilderness skills. Even with his developmental challenges, however, Robbie had learned some solid skills from his parents on the family's many camping trips. "Robbie's an old hand at it," George Mott told the *Biddeford-Saco Journal*. "He adjusts well to camp life and enjoys going to new places." In addition, Robbie had studied survival procedures at several boys' camps. It was possible that he would know to look for shelter or find a way to keep warm.

"This [camping] is nothing new to them," said Ruth Mott to the *Democrat & Chronicle*. "We haven't missed a year camping and it's nothing for both of them to hike all day." She told authorities that Robbie was very fond of Timmy and would take good care of his younger brother if they had encountered any kind of trouble.

Ordinarily, Mott said, the boys would know better than to leave the campsite without telling their parents or siblings. He added, "Both boys are adventurous, but not at suppertime."

Without his insulin medication, however, Robbie could become non-functional in a very short time. Ruth Mott told the media that "the boy would be in extreme difficulty if he did not receive insulin medication at regular intervals." He usually received two injections daily, and had not had one since Thursday morning. Nor was he carrying any insulin with him.

"If he didn't get it," George Mott added, "it's hard to tell what may have happened." Later he said to a reporter from United Press International, "If Robbie has an extra stress of tension or misses a meal, he is likely to go into a coma."

George suggested to the wardens that the boys probably wandered down the dirt road, the only way in or out of the campground to the rest of the park, and that they may have branched off onto one of several trails. He suggested the path to Sandy Stream Pond or to North Katahdin Lake.

Morning came, and no one had turned up any sign of the two missing boys. The Motts' dear friends from New Hampshire, the Grant family—parents of Martha's friend Bonnie—arrived at Roaring Brook to take Bonnie, Martha, and Greg home to stay with them until their brothers were found. The Motts and Grants had met the previous summer during a vacation at Acadia National Park, and they had formed a fast and lasting friendship that extended to visits and holidays throughout the year.

"They had six kids, so what were two more?" Martha said. She noted that their parents could not telephone them on a daily basis, as there were no easily available phones in the park. "We read the newspapers every day," she said. "By then it was national news. There were no lost children in those days."

The search-and-rescue team expanded significantly with first light: A Maine Forestry Department helicopter and a light plane provided by the Fish and Game Department began to canvas the area, their task hampered significantly by the dense foliage in Maine's lush northern forests. Soon a US Air Force helicopter from Loring Air Force Base joined the search, manned by an air rescue team and a paramedic with injectable insulin.

"The Air Force helicopter . . . is capable of pinpointing an object as small as a fountain pen," the *Democrat & Chronicle* reported. "The aircraft's spotter is suspended from an open door by a sling device and lowered to within a few feet of the ground when the crew finds a possible clue." This state-of-the-art technology, however, did not turn up so much as a sock that might lead to the missing boys.

The arrival of two bloodhounds from the Maine State Prison at Thomaston provided a welcome development as Saturday, July 31, dawned in the park. With fresh scent leading away from Roaring Brook Camp and plenty of clothing and belongings to provide a match, it seemed that the dogs would find the missing boys in no time. Indeed, the bloodhounds picked up the scent and took off out of the camp and into the woods. "We took them down along the brook, but eventually whatever scent they were on to apparently gave out, and we brought the dogs back," said Wight. While the hounds provided some direction as to the area the boys had crossed, they could not bring the search to a close.

The search party swelled to seventy-five people on Saturday, and continued to grow as the weekend progressed with no sign of the boys. "Warden Supervisor Dave Priest was soon directing a search effort unparalleled in Maine at that time," said Wight. "Within two days there were literally hundreds of searchers on the scene. The one-way road in and out of Roaring Brook Campground became clogged at times with vehicles transporting an army of searchers, and enough food and supplies to provide for them. . . . Civil Defense feeding units were set up to feed people around the clock." The American Red Cross sent food trucks and personnel as well to keep the teams fueled with hot meals and supplies, and to administer first aid to scratched and footsore searchers.

On Sunday, Maine Governor John H. Reed, monitoring the search from the state capital in Augusta, conferred with state officials and pledged that every available resource would be dedicated to the search. He authorized the state Fish and Game Department to use "all available state manpower" to find the two boys.

This directive doubled the search parties on Sunday. Seventy-one men and three officers of the Maine National Guard, a sixty-man detachment from Dow Air Force Base in Bangor, park rangers, game wardens, and some skilled civilians spread out across the landscape and walked ten feet apart in a grid pattern, watching the ground and the surrounding trees and brush for any scrap of clothing, shoe, or disturbance that could lead to a boy holed up to escape the evening chill. Supervisor Priest told the press that the activity remained concentrated within a three-mile radius of Roaring Brook Campground, an area of nine square miles.

"Officials are allowing only experienced personnel to help because of the rugged nature of the area," the *Democrat & Chronicle* reported. "Park authorities are reported to be discouraging additional campers from entering the Roaring Brook site in order to keep crowds and confusion at a minimum."

A Woodland Signature

Suddenly a whoop went up from one of the searchers. He had discovered a white birch tree with some recent disturbance: fresh scratching with a twig, spelling out the name "Robbie M." Now the search focused on the immediate area around the tree as several searchers ran back to the camp to find the Motts. They led George and Ruth to the tree along with Maine Warden Clayton Gifford, and the parents examined the carving closely. Ruth Mott believed that the final "e" in the carving looked very much like Robbie's handwriting.

"I'm certain this was Robbie," she declared. She immediately climbed to a high spot nearby and called out the names of her sons.

The wilderness responded with silence.

When search officials scrutinized the tree and its message, however, they could not come to a consensus on whether it could be a message from the missing boy, or a disturbing coincidence—or, worse, a prank. Some believed it had been carved in the last couple of days, while others concluded that it was older and already somewhat worn away by weather. Officials put out a call for a handwriting expert to examine the signature and determine if it had any resemblance to Robbie's writing, and the Motts called a family member to bring school papers written by the boy to the park to assist in the analysis. Days would pass, however, before all the elements would be available to make a determination of whether the lost boy had scrawled his name on the birch tree, and whether this could mean a narrowing of the search area.

By Sunday night, with no sign of the two boys, Ruth finally voiced her greatest fear: Perhaps the boys had been kidnapped. "Timmy was the type of child a person might well abduct," she said.

The Maine State Police took the proactive step to issue a statewide alert. "Deputy Sheriff Joseph Bartlett of Piscataqua County [*sic*—the county is Piscataquis, on the Piscataqua River] said there was always a possibility the boys were kidnapped but the alert was ordered 'more or less as a precautionary measure,'" the *Biddeford-Saco Journal* reported on Monday, August 2.

With sunset and the end of another day's searching, the Motts settled uneasily into their campsite for the fourth night since the boys' disappearance. They clung to one ray of hope: They had just heard that a nine-year-old boy missing in New York's Catskill Mountains had been found alive after he was lost for four days. Young Hershel Babad had wandered away from Camp B'nai Belz in Woodbridge, New York, to go blueberry picking. He saw a bird that caught his fancy, followed it into the woods, and could not find his way back to camp. Hershel emerged scratched and bruised from his ordeal and very hungry, but essentially unharmed.

If one child could survive several days in the woods, perhaps Robbie and Timmy could as well. The Motts ended the day with new hope in their hearts. Ruth Mott told hometown reporter Bill Claiborne that her son's need for insulin had passed by now, because he would have used up the sugar in his system during the first night in the woods. "If he could wake up Saturday morning,

I feel he'll be all right," she said. "He could stay alive as long as any healthy child could."

As Monday morning arrived and search activity picked up at first light, the effort expanded further, with Governor Reed authorizing Fish and Game Department Commissioner Ronald T. Speers to deploy twenty additional wardens to aid in the operation. "The governor extended his sympathy to the boys' parents," the *Biddeford-Saco Journal* reported.

Monday afternoon brought no new clues on the fourth day of full-scale searching. Supervisor Priest conferred with doctors to weigh the efficacy of continuing to assume that the boys could be alive, and their perspective convinced him to continue the effort. "He said the search would continue until there is some major development on the whereabouts of the youngsters," Mike Michaud of the *Nashua Telegraph* wrote. Michaud concluded on an ominous note: "He predicted it might take a couple of weeks."

Then on Monday evening, searchers found a set of footprints about three miles from Roaring Brook Camp on Windy Road, heading northeast toward Katahdin Lake. The prints matched the brothers' shoes and their sizes. Military personnel and civilian searchers now focused their attention on the area to the northeast, hoping to pick up more clues the boys may have left along the trail. More prints came to light, but they did not lead to the Mott brothers. Perhaps the boys had left the road and tried to bushwhack through the woods, or maybe the ground was simply harder up the road. Whatever the reason, the prints did not reveal any more clues.

Now friends and family members began to arrive to help bolster the Motts' ability to cope with the prolonged search. The children's two uncles, Raymond and John Woolston of Livonia, New York, and their pastor, the Reverend Dr. Carlton B. Allen, joined them at Roaring Brook Camp to wait with them for news, however scant, of the boys' whereabouts.

Officials, Experts, and Crackpots

Passing the four-day mark on Monday—the time that Hershel Babad had survived in the Catskills—became the first major benchmark in the prolonged search effort. Now the Motts and the searchers hung their hopes on another familiar north-woods story: the often-told true tale of Donn Fendler, a twelve-year-old Boy Scout from Rye, New York, who survived eight days in the Maine wilderness in 1939.

Fendler applied his Scout training to stay alive, and Robbie Mott had had wilderness survival training as well. The Motts clung to whatever hope they were offered.

Tuesday morning, August 3, brought the arrival of the state's adjutant general, Major General Edwin W. Heywood, and Fish and Game Commissioner Speers to the command center of the search. They came to observe the process and to gather firsthand information for a report to Governor Reed, who had become concerned at the length of the search and its lack of results. Heywood and Speers "were not dissatisfied with the way the search was going," reporter Michaud noted, "and added that search director David Priest would get more manpower if he needed or wanted it."

Priest, however, turned down the offer. "He wants the search party limited to about 300 men because more than this number would be too difficult to control," the report in the *Nashua Telegram* said.

Nonetheless, the ranks of the searchers swelled to nearly four hundred on Tuesday, even as a handwriting expert arrived on the scene to examine the carving found on the white birch tree. Old Town Police Chief Otie Labree, formerly a detective with the Maine State Police, compared Robbie's handwriting on school papers supplied by the family to the crudely scratched letters on the tree. His conclusion: "No comparison." The scratched signature was merely a coincidence—or someone's idea of a cruel joke.

On Wednesday, August 4, Maine State Police heard from a self-described "recognized extra sensory perception expert in Scarborough," who instructed them to search an area northeast of the campsite. Police conveyed this dubious advice to the wardens on site, and they dutifully canvassed the area, which contained a waterfall that had a slim chance of providing a hazard for children. This "clue" turned up nothing, however, and the wardens returned to their methodical, fact-based operations.

There was nothing left to do but check, recheck, and check again, covering all the areas the searchers had already covered. "I don't know how many times they have looked but the boys could be missed," said Millinocket Police Chief Richard Rideout on Wednesday, August 4, the sixth full day of the search. "Some of that swamp grass is so high and thick you would have to practically step on them."

Worse, heavy rains had begun to fall midweek, chilling the personnel and turning the search into a sloshy mess.

Daybreak on Thursday, August 5, saw wardens, baffled by the lack of clues, breaking up a number of beaver dams in streams within the search area, lowering the water level by as much as two feet. With the dams gone, the wardens could look under the now-shallow water to see if one or both of the boys had fallen into a stream and been carried by the current until they became lodged under a dam.

An anonymous veteran searcher noted, "When we do that, you know we've hit rock bottom."

Reporters asked Priest why he had not ordered a dragging operation in the area's creeks and ponds. "The pond near where the boys were last seen is shallow enough to see the bottom from a boat," he said, "so there's no point dragging that." Most of the park's creeks had only a trickle of water in them in July and August, so even little Timmy could cross on foot.

Even without a single clue coming to light, Ruth Mott remained hopeful. "They could still be moving in the wrong direction, but I think they could stay alive," she told Claiborne of the Rochester paper. "There's a lot to eat and plenty of water. . . . I just hope that the search will go on. I couldn't stand the thought of going home without knowing one way or the other. It's bad enough having to wait here and not know if they're suffering or what has happened to them."

Help from Home

"The days continued," wrote Eric Wight in *Life and Death in the North Woods*. "A week went by; no clues. Searchers were becoming exhausted and were replaced by fresh ones from as far away as New York State. The terrain around Mount Katahdin has never been called gentle—beautiful, perhaps, but not gentle—and a new pair of boots could be worn out in a week. Searchers sprained ankles and received other assorted injuries. The nights were cold, and on several, there was frost. . . . Supervisor Dave Priest, however, remained unflappable. He insisted they were here somewhere—we just had not found the spot. We did, however, all agree that by now we were undoubtedly looking for two bodies."

By this time, the Motts' friends and coworkers in Rochester, New York, were aching for a way to help the couple and their children. President of Xerox Joe Wilson took it upon himself to charter a plane and send a total of eighty-two Xerox employee volunteers to aid in the search effort. In his characteristic style, Wilson did this with no fanfare—no company newsletter articles or announcements to the company's workforce, and no trumpeting in the press.

James Carr, community relations director for Xerox, coordinated the company's involvement in the search. He and his team screened more than three hundred volunteers from its workforce, sending only men with woods experience who were under thirty years old and in excellent physical condition, noted Chief Game Warden Maynard Marsh. Xerox used "excellent judgment and sent fine woodsmen to aid us," he told Claiborne of the *Democrat &*

Chronicle. Xerox paid all of the men their full salaries and picked up all the expenses of their participation in the search.

Rochester's other behemoth corporation, Eastman Kodak Company, also lent a hand at the request of one of its employees (whose name is lost to history), who went to the same church as the Mott family. Kodak footed the bill to fly ten members of Twelve Corners Presbyterian Church to assist in the search. The volunteers spent several days serving on teams and scouring the woods for clues.

On Saturday, August 7, another not-quite-plausible lead drifted into the camp. Fishermen in the park reported that on the previous Wednesday, August 4, they saw two boys resembling the Mott brothers about fifteen miles from the Roaring Brook Camp. Perhaps the fishermen had not heard about the missing boys until days after they saw these two youngsters, or maybe they did not cross paths with any rangers or wardens during the course of their fishing trip in the backcountry. By the time this word reached the search directors, however, they discounted it out of hand. They reasoned that the two boys could not possibly have walked that far, and left it at that.

No Longer a Rescue Mission

Sunday marked the ninth day since the boys went missing, and officials had no choice but to downgrade the effort from a rescue mission to one of recovering the boys' bodies. The mood changed significantly as groups of volunteers began to depart for home: Half of the Xerox volunteers flew back to Rochester, while forty-three remained to help on Monday. They left Millinocket Sunday evening and were transported by air to Roaring Brook Camp, landing there at 11:20 that night.

On Monday morning, August 9, wardens quickly organized and dispatched the Xerox volunteers in groups of twelve, spreading them through the nine-square-mile grid around the campground and the neighboring ponds. This left just seven Xerox volunteers in the campsite. Morning dragged on into afternoon with the group receiving no instructions or assignment. This last group—Ronald Cade, James Gastonguay, Terry Kimbrough, David Kirker, Jerry Myers, Richard Nagel, and Ryland "Ry" Rogers—finally got the beleaguered wardens' attention and asked to be sent into the woods to participate in the search.

The Xerox searchers knew that they had only a limited time to help. Earlier the same day, Maine Health and Welfare Commissioner Dean Fisher, MD, had issued a report stating that Robbie and Timmy could not have survived in the Maine backcountry for more than ten days. Fisher had consulted with top medical authorities in Maine, as well as the children's family physician, Dr. Richard Meltzer in Rochester. "I believe there are no imaginable circumstances under which either of the children could be expected to survive beyond ten days," the report read. "For all practical purposes there is no reason to assume survival beyond one week. With the information available on the conditions of Robbie Mott . . . there does not seem to be any conceivable set of circumstances which would have permitted his survival for more than a week."

Fisher reported that he had looked very closely at Timmy's ability to survive, whether or not Robbie was still with him. "It is somewhat more difficult to feel equally as certain about the probable length of survival of three-year-old Timothy," he reported. "However, even in his case it is impossible to imagine circumstances which would have permitted survival beyond a week."

Commissioner Speers and Maine Civil Defense Director Lester Stanley drove to the park from Augusta, the state capital, to review Fisher's report with them and break the news that the boys were very likely no longer alive. They joined the Motts in their trailer along with Priest, Chief Game Warden Maynard Marsh, and Jack Shaw, Maine deputy chief game warden.

The officials explained that a search would continue in hopes of recovering the bodies of the two boys, but this would involve only about thirty wardens, and it would not be conducted with the urgency of the previous ten days' activity. Searching would continue "for as long as Priest felt it was advisable," the *Democrat & Chronicle* reported.

The Motts took the news calmly, as the prolonged search had already fomented the idea in their own minds that Robbie and Timmy would not emerge from this ordeal alive. George Mott asked one last favor of Commissioner Speers, however: that he follow up on the lead, however unlikely, from the fishermen who reported a sighting of two boys far from Roaring Brook Camp several days before. The Motts had "all but discounted" the lead, but they knew that if the boys were never found, they would wonder about the fishermen's sighting for the rest of their lives.

After all the officials left their trailer, the Motts emerged and walked to the mobile field kitchen, where search crews had received meals and gathered in between shifts to share information. Here the Motts spoke with George's coworkers and family friends, thanking them for all of their efforts in a first step toward coming to terms with the loss of their two sons. They also talked with members of the press, asking them to thank all of the people who had assisted in the search, as well as those who had offered emotional support, condolences, and donations throughout the massive effort. Ruth Mott asked that monetary contributions be sent to the Maine Civil Defense fund in support of the local unit in Millinocket.

The End of the Search

With just hours left before the search operation would become a scaled-down recovery mission, a warden assigned the last group of seven Xerox employees to an area that had already been examined by a number of other parties. Group members later told the media that they had been assembled "almost as an afterthought," as wardens assumed that the group would turn up nothing at all. The Xerox group remained undaunted, however, and the seven men set off up the dirt road to the Katahdin Lake Trail, the area in which searchers had found footprints a few days earlier.

Game wardens and a Great Northern Paper Company timber cruiser directed the party's search efforts. The seven volunteers spread out until they were about ten feet apart, and walked in a line along the edges of the trail as rain poured from the sky, filling every impression in the dirt road and path and soaking their boots.

Late in the afternoon, Ronald Cade spotted something on a little hill, not quite as high as a man's shoulder. He stepped out of line for a closer look, separated the branches and woodland detritus with both hands, and knew in an instant that he had found the boys.

"The hill had a depression in the top that was big enough for two boys to have a little nest," Martha explained. "They had protection from the area, where they could lie with each other side by side during the night."

Ry Rogers described the scene to the *Democrat & Chronicle*'s Bill Claiborne as "a wooded knoll . . . a little glen with lots of cedars." Later he added, "The tree trunks were ten to fifteen feet apart. They were very obvious and couldn't be missed."

Priest told the media that search parties passed the knoll several times on the first night of the search, but missed the boys because low shrubs and other vegetation hid their bodies. It was also possible that the boys were not in the knoll during the first search of the area, and that they came to rest there hours later. Even the Air Force helicopter had missed them because of the dense forest canopy above the knoll.

The team rushed out of the woods to the dirt access road and sent word to the wardens. News of the discovery reached the Motts in a matter of minutes.

George Mott's reaction was concise. "Thank God they have been found," he said.

Now wardens could piece together a possible scenario that had led to the brothers' untimely end. The boys had walked down the dirt road to the Katahdin Lake Trail—the route where their footprints were found days earlier—and started down the trail to the lake. How and why they left the trail itself and became so hidden in the brush will never be known; perhaps Robbie attempted to shield himself and his brother from the cold during their first or second unprotected night in the wilderness.

"We think they probably saw an animal and tried to follow it to get a better look," said Martha. "Then they just got lost in the woods."

It was also possible that Robbie felt the effects of his lack of insulin during that first night, lay down in some brush, and never rose again. "Most diabetics could live on one shot a day—I was diabetic also, and I did—but having missed his evening shot, he was probably near comatose by morning," Martha said. Timmy stayed close to his brother until he, too, succumbed to the chilly night.

Medical examiner Norman H. Nickerson, MD, lost no time in arriving at the scene and examining the bodies before they were transported to a funeral home in Millinocket. He confirmed that the boys had been dead for "some time," but his cursory examination did not reveal how long ago they had died, or the exact cause of death.

Hearing that the boys had been found, Xerox president Joe Wilson once again authorized a chartered plane, this time to bring the children's uncles and the family pastor back to the park to aid the Mott family. The plane arrived in Millinocket at 6:10 p.m., just two hours after the boys were located.

Within hours, official condolences began to arrive. "My personal sympathy and that of Maine Governor John H. Reed, and I am sure the sympathy of everyone in Maine, is extended to Dr. and Mrs. Mott at this time," said Speers. "We are truly grieved at this tragedy and hope that the intensity and effort put into this search has been an indication of our feeling for them."

There were still loose ends to tie up. The Motts declined an offer from Xerox to fly them home, opting instead to drive with the help of their friend Michael Vince, who would bring home their trailer. They remained in Baxter State Park for two more days to await the medical examiner's report.

Dr. George Chase of Eastern Maine General Hospital in Bangor performed the autopsy on August 10. He determined that the boys had been dead for at least five or six days and probably longer, though he believed that they survived their first night in the woods. He could not confirm that Robbie's diabetes had played a role in his death, or which of the boys had died first. Chase did some routine testing to find out if the boys had found anything to eat in the woods. Their stomachs contained roots and berries, proof that they had used Robbie's survival skills in an attempt to withstand their time in the forest.

"We'll continue studying some body tissue, but whatever answers we get will be just academic," he said.

He did confirm that the boys had not come to harm at the hands of an unknown person. "They were not scratched and their clothing was not torn," he said, noting that this proved there was no foul play. "It doesn't appear that they traveled very far."

An examination of the knoll provided some additional information. When they reached the knoll, the boys tried to light a fire, and eventually fell asleep, and Robbie may have lapsed into a coma. Temperatures in the low fifties may have led to Timmy's death by exposure.

The Motts drove home to Penfield, a suburb of Rochester, where their friends and family waited to help them move forward from the desperate days of hope, despair, and eventual resignation.

"One thing I remember, after we got home," Martha said. "It was a couple of days later. Dad gathered us in the living room on the sofa and tearfully told us to remember that they were in heaven, and they were safe and happy now." Tears came to her eyes at the memory. "He said that Robbie would have had more trouble in this life than he deserved, and that Timmy was too perfect for this world, so God wanted him in heaven with Him.

We would have to go on without them and be happy for them, more than missing them."

The Motts moved on. George became very involved with helping the church prepare the space for a new pipe organ, and he pursued his hobby of fine woodworking in addition to his career at Xerox. He and Ruth still took the family camping every summer, including an extended trip to the southwestern United States in 1966 to visit all the national parks and monuments there. Bonnie Grant and her brother, Mike, often accompanied them.

They came together in northern Maine one more time. The landowner of the woods adjacent to Baxter State Park gave the Motts permission to scatter the boys' ashes there, in a forest like the one they had loved so well in their short lives.

CHAPTER 2

Looking for Roy Bradeen

NOT EVERYONE'S DEATH IN A NATIONAL PARK BECOMES A MEDIA event. Some people push their bodies beyond the limits of their own endurance, suffering a heart attack, stroke, or a more unusual medical issue—things that don't necessarily rise to the media's attention. Others simply go unreported. The park staff invariably knows that a fatality has taken place and is usually involved in removing a victim's body from the park, but the death itself may not become a news story.

The passing of Roy Bradeen, for example, is noted on a list compiled on a website called Katahdin Outdoors, a useful but apparently orphaned site that appears to have been maintained by someone on the Baxter State Park staff in the early 2000s. The site tells us that Roy Bradeen and his wife, Laura (Perro), owned and ran Kidney Pond Camps in the late 1920s and 1930s, and that Roy met an untimely end in October 1927 or 1937, when he drowned in Kidney Pond.

Bradeen was the first person identified by name to lose his life in the park, so it seemed that there should be considerable information available about what happened to him—especially since he owned Kidney Pond Camps and was probably a well-known citizen in the area.

The search to discover exactly what happened to Bradeen took me on a circuitous route, so I thought it might interest readers to follow along and get an idea of the challenges we researchers face in finding the truth in history.

One page of KatahdinOutdoors.com, a list of fatalities in the park, places Bradeen's death in October 1927, and notes that he may have had a heart attack or drowned—but another page tells stories of rangers and personnel in the 1940s, and specifically notes, "In 1937, Roy was drowned in Kidney Pond."

The ambiguities about the date are only part of the unusual nature of this piece of information. Drowning in the pond seems like an odd way for Roy to die, especially if you understand a bit more about Kidney Pond campground and its history.

The original hunting camp sprang from the enthusiasm for the Maine backcountry of the appropriately named Hunt family. Back in 1832, courageous and intrepid settler William Hunt chose an area on the eastern branch of the Penobscot River, near Stacyville, to clear and make his home. Generations later, two of his grandsons, Irvin O. and Lyman Hunt, set up their own sporting camp on Nesowadnehunk Stream on a spot known as Indian Pitch. Here in summer and fall, they hosted outdoor sportsmen who came to hunt, fish, and climb the area's mountains, and in winter the Hunt brothers remained there and hunted on their own.

Apparently these two gentlemen developed quite a reputation as backcountry guides, for their camp's popularity grew so much that they determined they needed to expand their capacity. The result was a second Hunt's Camp, founded and open for business in 1902—and one of their earliest visitors was Percival P. Baxter, the most passionate advocate for preservation of Maine's north woods and waters and the future fifty-third governor of Maine.

Not much is written about these early days at the camps, although Frank H. Sleeper's book, *Baxter State Park and the Allagash River*, provides many photos of rugged men in this heavily forested setting. We do know that the camps provided a truly rustic outdoor experience, with spaces for tents, clearings in which campers could build cooking fires, and outhouses that reminded visitors how much they loved their plumbing at home. This was a far cry from the concept of camps Downeast, where wealthy families made the trip to Bar Harbor to "rusticate" in lavish homes and drive their horses and buggies along carriage trails through what would become Acadia National Park. In the north woods, turn-of-the-century camping meant sleeping on the ground, battling blackflies, and burying one's own waste—a true opportunity to reunite with nature on every conceivable level.

By 1909, according to an advertisement Irving Hunt placed in the Bangor and Aroostook Railroad newsletter *In the Maine Woods*, accommodations had gentrified at the camp. "Cozy camps, the best of beds, and the best of table fare," the ad proclaimed, "Fresh vegetables from our own garden, fresh eggs, fresh milk and butter. The purest spring water and a large ice house are on the premises." All this could be had via "a delightful trip up the beautiful West branch of the Penobscot [River] to the mouth of Sourdnahunk Stream and up the stream three miles to Kidney Pond."

In 1918, Irving Hunt took on a partner, a man named Bradeen, whom we can assume was Roy Bradeen himself. Irving extricated himself from the business by 1921, perhaps moving on to a comfortable retirement in his home in Hampden, Maine, while Bradeen took on a new partner—a person named Clifford—and changed the name to Kidney Pond Camps. By this time the flourishing camp no longer required that guests bring their own sleeping accommodations: Kidney Pond Camps sported log cabins, new hunting lodges, telephone service, and indoor plumbing. As more and more visitors owned automobiles, the camp made arrangements for a driving route all the way from Greenville to the Sourdnahunk Stream with a crossing over the Great Northern Paper Company's enormous dam. At the stream, camp staff met visitors to take them to the camp in a horse-drawn wagon. "No Walking," the advertisements promised.

Roy Bradeen married Laura Perro in 1922, and Katahdin Outdoors.com tells us that in 1925 or 1926, the Bradeens became partners in the business. Clifford was no longer mentioned in the advertising, which now touted Bradeen & Bradeen as the management team.

Then something happened to Roy. A heart attack, a drowning . . . the record simply wasn't clear. While writing books about deaths in national and state parks has made me aware that even the most sure-footed and experienced outdoorsmen and women can make tiny mistakes that cost them their lives, it seemed strange that Bradeen should die in the pond that had flanked a camp he had owned for nearly two decades.

I couldn't imagine that someone who was undoubtedly well known in the community in and around the park—including the town of Millinocket, which serves as the park's headquarters and entrance town sixteen miles away from the southernmost entrance—would pass away without a single mention in the press, but my searches through digitized newspapers turned up nary a line about Roy Bradeen. So I made a trip from my home in western New York State up to the public library in Bangor, Maine, where the *Bangor Daily News*—one of the only newspapers in America that has not digitized its archives—resides in five cabinets full of spools of microfilm. The newspapers in October 1937 held not a drop of ink on the subject of Bradeen's death, though wily local history librarian Betsy Paradis did find a notice that Laura Bradeen remarried a man named Randolph P. Latno on May 19, 1938. Laura continued to use the name Bradeen for her business affairs, however, referring to herself in advertising as "(Mrs.) Roy Bradeen," carrying on the brand legacy she and her first husband had built for a generation.

Could the date of death be incorrect? To find out, I turned to death records at FamilySearch.org, the venerable genealogy database managed by the Church of Jesus Christ of Latter-Day

Saints. It turns out that Leroy Bradeen—his full name—is listed as dying on October 8, 1933. The national Social Security Index agrees with this, and Roy's tombstone, in Butterfield Cemetery in Prentiss, Penobscot County (another discovery by Betsy Paradis), states: "In loving memory to my husband Roy Bradeen/To have known him was to have loved him/1882–1933." The cemetery's record lists Roy's wife as Laura Perro, so we know for certain that this is the same man.

Why the discrepancy? It's hard to know what kind of records were kept at the park back in the 1930s, but we can be nearly certain that they were handwritten at best, and perhaps merely anecdotal. Indeed, Sleeper's book notes that a 1936 print advertisement still lists the camp management as Bradeen & Bradeen, even though Roy had been dead three years. Laura undoubtedly had sound business reasons for doing this: In the 1930s, a young widow running a backcountry camp on her own in the wilds of Maine may have attracted a slew of attention, and at least some of it may have come from people who would attempt to take advantage of her.

With the correct date in hand, I made my way up to Millinocket to do a deep dive into the newspapers there . . . and came up empty. Trudy Wyman, the Millinocket Historical Society curator, searched the town's records and the newspapers she had on hand and did not find any mention of Roy Bradeen. The Millinocket Public Library, now struggling and staffed almost entirely by volunteers, contains no newspapers dated before 1941, and all of the papers filed there are fragile, original paper copies stacked consecutively in flat archival boxes. Whatever may have been written in Millinocket about the passing of Roy Bradeen in 1933 has been lost.

I turned to the state of Maine for a death certificate for Leroy Bradeen, so I could at least be sure of how he died as well as when. Once I had explained my purpose in a letter to the vital records office, the record of a death from October 8, 1933, arrived in short order. Sure enough, Leroy Bradeen had died from "accidental drowning from canoe."

Here's the thing, though—when I'd visited the Bangor Public Library a month earlier, I had believed Roy had died in 1937, so I searched only the papers for that year. Knowing now exactly when Roy died, I corresponded one more time with Betsy Paradis at the Bangor Public Library, and she searched the *Bangor Daily News* and another paper, the *Bangor Daily Commercial*.

Here, finally, we found the full story, in the *Commercial* on October 10, 1933.

Details of the drowning at Kidney Pond late Sunday of Roy Bradeen, 50, proprietor of sporting camps, were received late Monday upon the return of Sheriff Thomas Foulkes and Deputy Lloyd Hoxie, who went to Kidney Pond Monday morning upon learning of the drowning.

His canoe capsizing shortly after he had started from York's sporting camp to cross Kidney Pond to his own camps, Bradeen was drowned a short distance from the shore and his body was recovered by searchers Monday noon.

Bradeen, accompanied by his dog, left the York camps shortly after 5 o'clock, and when he failed to show up at his place at 7, his wife telephoned to York's to see if he were still there.

Informed that he had left, she became alarmed, and with Fred Daley and Miss Ethel Scott, began a search for him, which continued throughout the night.

Meantime, Bradeen's dog, which escaped the fate of its master, returned late at night to the York camps and some hours afterwards the canoe was discovered.

Monday morning Charles Dalcy and Fred Roberts, game warden, instituted a hunt for the body of the missing man, and found it not far off shore.

Bradeen was one of the best known sporting camp owners in this section and his untimely death will be deeply regretted in many homes.

Another notice (which calls him "Roy Bragdon") appeared the following Thursday as the Bradeen family held his funeral, including a Masonic service, and laid Roy to rest in the Prentiss cemetery.

The question remains, of course, why a man who spent sixteen summers living at the south end of Kidney Pond should suddenly meet his end by capsizing a canoe. Unfortunate accidents happen every day, however, and we can't always determine every fact about them when they do. At least we were able to clear up the ambiguities about the death of Roy Bradeen, and set the historic record right after it had been contorted and almost lost.

And what of Kidney Pond Camps? It continued to flourish in the hands of other owners, the most notable of which was the Norris family, which took over the concession in the 1950s. Throughout much of the twentieth century, the Norrises made Kidney Pond campground a beloved favorite of Baxter State Park visitors, many of whom made their reservations as far out as a year in advance. In 1987, however, the state of Maine closed this last private concession in the park, and Steve and Nancy Norris moved on to open The Pines Lodge on Sysladobsis Lake in 1992. The camp still stands on Kidney Pond, but its many amenities—including flush toilets—have been stripped out of it to bring it back to the rustic spirit of its original purpose: an opportunity to commune directly with nature, with as few modern conveniences as possible between the camper and the wonders of Baxter State Park.

Shooting Accident at Kidney Pond

As it turned out, Roy Bradeen would not be the last to die at Kidney Pond Camps. When Laura Bradeen left Kidney Pond in 1945, the Doxsee family of Meriden, Connecticut, assumed the lease. Oscar Doxsee became the owner, and he and his son, Marshall, worked at the camp throughout the season.

In the summer of 1950, a black bear gave some of the campers significant scares by hanging around close to the camp. It was not uncommon in parks across the country in the 1950s for camp kitchen staff to throw out scraps in open dumping sites for bears and other animals to eat, or to leave food waste out in trash cans that were all too easy for bears to knock over and empty onto the ground. "Although there was no television provided for entertainment, the park had a nightly 'show' for visitors: bears feeding on garbage," noted the 2008 book *Wilderness Partners: Buzz Caverly and Baxter State Park*, written by Phyllis Austin. "Rangers were happy to direct people to the dumps at dusk to watch the bruins paw through stinking leftovers and rubbish."

Bears unwittingly provided amusement for campers and other visitors as long as they kept their distance from one another, and there were no major confrontations between the animals and campers in Baxter State Park. In August 1967, every park across the country became aware of the potential danger of this practice on the dramatic night that became known as the "Night of the Grizzlies" in Glacier National Park. Two young women in two different areas of the national park in northwestern Montana were killed and partially devoured by grizzly bears within hours of one another, in what finally was determined to be an astonishing coincidence. Both bears, habituated to scavenging in human camps for food, made an unexpected leap to believing humans were actually food themselves. The bears were captured and destroyed, and national parks closed and cleaned up their dumps.

Kidney Pond Camps undoubtedly had such a dump, but as long as the bears showed up only at the appointed time to raid the trash heap, they were considered to be nothing worse than highly entertaining. When a black bear began skulking around close to camp at other times of the day, however, it became a worrisome prospect for camp management. Black bears are the smaller of the bear species in the contiguous United States, but at two to three hundred pounds each, a black bear can overpower a person and cause major injuries, particularly if the bear sees the human as a threat.

Young Marshall Doxsee, who was thirty-two, took it upon himself to police the area and get rid of the bear. He kept his shotgun handy and waited for his opportunity to dispatch the animal quickly and cleanly.

On the evening of June 22, 1950, young Ethel Pease, an eighteen-year-old working as a summer waitress at Kidney Pond Camps, left her cabin with her fourteen-year-old sister, Dorothy, to make her way to the outdoor toilet. Another waitress, Edith McNaughton of Grafton, Massachusetts, came along with them.

Ethel had just graduated from high school in Portland with "second highest girl's honors," according to the *Boston Globe*, and she had gained some experience as a server at private parties in Portland before becoming a waitress at the popular wilderness camp. Ethel and Dorothy had ten other brothers and sisters at home with their parents, Mr. and Mrs. Henry Pease, and in the coming fall, Ethel was set to enter the Maine General Hospital School of Nursing in Portland.

While the girls were using the restroom, campers alerted Marshall Doxsee that they had glimpsed a bear lurking just beyond the trees near the camp. Doxsee stopped at his quarters to get his rifle and ammunition, and set off in the direction the campers indicated.

As Ethel and Dorothy completed their ablutions and began to return to their cabin, Doxsee saw a rustling in the woods and spotted a shape moving along the trail toward the camp. He didn't hesitate to take his shot, and his aim was true.

But the movement did not come from a bear at all. Ethel Pease crumpled to the ground with a bullet in her back, amid the screams of her sister and friend.

"Game Warden Alexander Cummings said ... Miss Pease was killed instantly," the Associated Press reported. Shortly afterward, "members of a sheriff's party killed a bear nearby."

Doxsee said only that he thought Pease was the bear.

After two weeks of investigation, the court in Dover-Foxcroft, Maine, issued a manslaughter warrant signed by Piscataquis County Sheriff Harold True for Doxsee's arrest. Doxsee was taken into custody with a $5,000 bond on July 6, and he pleaded innocent to the charge.

What transpired over the next two months did not make it into court records, but on September 13, Doxsee appeared in superior court and changed his plea to guilty of the manslaughter charge. He was sentenced to serve no prison time and to pay a $700 fine.

The Associated Press summed up this verdict eloquently the following day: "Killing Girl for Bear in Maine Costs $700."

CHAPTER 3

Split Seconds: Lightning Strikes

IT'S SUCH AN EASY PHRASE TO TOSS INTO A CONVERSATION: "YOU have better odds of being struck by lightning than of . . ." any number of things, from winning the lottery to contracting the Zika virus. A lightning strike seems to be the most distant and unlikely event in any person's life, so we use it freely as a benchmark for the remotest of possibilities.

The statistics about lightning strikes, however, reveal some surprising facts. They're a lot more common than you may think.

Lightning bolts strike the United States about 25 million times every year, or about forty-eight times per minute, according to the National Severe Storms Laboratory, a division of the National Oceanic and Atmospheric Administration. It may seem like the odds that any individual could be struck by lightning ought to be pretty high, but the National Weather Service (NWS) says otherwise: The chance of an individual in the US being killed or injured by lightning during a given year is one in 1,083,000, based on an average of the number of lightning strikes from 2007 to 2016. When we assume that the average person now lives to be 80 years old, the likelihood gets disturbingly better: The odds of being hit at some point in a lifetime drop to one in 13,500. Those are much better odds than winning the Powerball (one in 292 million) or the Mega Millions jackpot (one in 259 million), or even of contracting Zika on a trip to Rio de Janeiro (one in 250,000).

As scary as these ratios may be, the fact is that the actual number of people who are struck by lightning in the United States each year is quite low. On average from 2007 to 2016, only thirty people per year die of a lightning strike, and another three hundred are injured but survive. Even the longer-term figures serve to assuage fear a bit more: from 1987 to 2016, lightning killed just forty-seven people per year. "Only about 10 percent of people who are struck by lightning are killed, leaving 90 percent with various degrees of disability," the NWS reports.

None of these figures take into account the destructive power of a particularly curious phenomenon in atmospheric science: the largely unexplained occurrence of ball lightning. According to firsthand accounts recorded by the news media, this strange weather event may or may not have manifested in Baxter State Park on August 24, 1968, when two dozen people felt the effects of explosive lightning in Chimney Pond Campground . . . and one of those people died.

For decades, science dismissed the mysterious wonder known as "ghost lights" or "fireballs," along with the claims of sky-watchers who said they had seen other unidentified flying objects, giving them the same level of legitimacy as posthumous sightings of Elvis Presley or fuzzy photos of Bigfoot. How could there be a weather phenomenon that produced a ball of lightning, one that varied from the size of a pea to an eight-foot orb of static electricity? How could lightning linger long enough to produce a ball—one that might even rocket its way around a canyon, materialize spontaneously inside a military plane, or remain long enough to scorch dozens of people?

Despite the skepticism of scientists, people have reported the occurrence of this singularity for hundreds of years. National Geographic.com explored the concept back in 2006, asking John Abrahamson, chemistry professor at the University of Canterbury in Christchurch, New Zealand, about the historical record. "[There are] around 10,000 written accounts of observations covering many countries with similar properties recurring in many observations," he told writer Brian Handwerk. "All this points to a phenomenon which is repeatable and justifies a single label."

As recently as the first decade of the twenty-first century, however, science had no explanation why one thunderstorm might generate a series of split seconds of conventional lightning, while another creates a lingering sphere. Graham K. Hubler, a physicist at the US Naval Research Laboratory in Washington, DC, told NationalGeographic.com, "I don't think anyone knows what it is. . . . Most scientists feel that the proper model hasn't been found yet."

At the time, however, roughly one in 150 people believed they had seen ball lightning, including Hubler himself. As he waited for a thunderstorm to pass in an open-sided park pavilion when he was eighteen, he saw a glowing ball, just about the size of a tennis ball, hovering not far from where he stood. "It's extraordinary—you're so startled that you remember it for the rest of your life," he told Handwerk. "It drifted along a few feet above the ground, but when it came inside [the pavilion], it dropped down to the ground and skittered along the floor. It made lots of gyrations or oscillations and a hissing sound like boiling water. When it went out the other side, it climbed back up [several feet off the ground]."

Even years later when he became a scientist, people regarded Hubler with a dubious eye when he described the mysterious occurrence. "They thought I was crazy, so I stopped talking about it," he said.

Hubler was hardly the only person with an interest. Eyewitness accounts have accumulated since the 1600s, and descriptions of strange phenomena that match the behavior of ball lightning date back to ancient oral accounts in the Mapuche culture in south-central Chile and Argentina. The stories describe beings called *anchimayen*, which can transform themselves into balls of intensely bright light to inhabit the corpses of dead children. Back in 1638 in Widecombe-in-the-Moor in Dartmoor, England, a ball of lightning suddenly invaded the church of St. Pancras during what became known as the Great Thunderstorm. The ball, described as being eight feet across, swept into the church through a window in the middle of a service with three hundred people attending. The lightning tore off part of the roof, rebounded against the walls, and killed four people, injuring as many as sixty others. Later, clergy and others attributed the destructive ball to a visit by the devil himself. Apparently a local gambler called Jan Reynolds was believed to have entered into a pact with the devil to increase his card-playing winnings, allowing Beelzebub to take his soul if Reynolds ever fell asleep in church. To the chagrin of his fellow worshippers, Reynolds dozed a bit on October 21, 1638, and they believed the devil took his due.

Ship captains in the eighteenth century reported lightning that descended upon their crafts in the form of a ball, shattering the mast or setting it on fire. These and other accounts led Georg Richmann, a professor in Saint Petersburg, Russia, to build an apparatus in 1753 that was not dissimilar to the kite Benjamin Franklin used to harness the power of electricity a year earlier. In the middle of a thunderstorm, Richmann's contraption attracted a ball of lightning that traveled down the kite string and collided with the professor's forehead. It knocked him backwards and killed him, leaving him with a large red spot on his forehead, singed clothing, and exploded shoes. The ball tore the room's door off its hinges and split the doorframe on its way out of the building.

There's no way to guess how many instances of ball lightning went unreported over the ensuing centuries, but whenever groups of people—especially men of science—witnessed the strange phenomenon, their reports became part of lightning history. Multiple glowing orbs appeared above the Hall of Engineering at the School of Mines in Golden, Colorado, in November 1894.

The city of Ouralsk in what is now Kazakhstan received a "dazzlingly brilliant ball of fire" in 1901, which entered a house and did significant damage before lifting and carrying the stovepipe out through a smashed window. In World War II, pilots who routinely flew in or just below clouds saw small, rapidly moving balls of light that they eventually dubbed "foo fighters." In at least one instance, the ball entered a military plane and hovered inside it.

Despite all of these accounts from credible sources, however, the field of atmospheric physics had no clear explanations for the conditions that caused ball lightning, or even what it actually might be. Scientists collecting information about the sightings did come up with a fairly reliable list of characteristics for the glowing orbs, which at least helped to screen out the true crackpots while compiling data on real occurrences:

1. The balls are usually spheres or pear-shaped, with fuzzy edges.

2. They range widely in size, from a single centimeter across all the way to eight inches. (The report in 1638 of an eight-foot ball has been dismissed as exaggeration.)

3. They are not blindingly bright, matching an average light bulb in intensity, so people can actually look at them head-on for a few seconds.

4. They can last from a single second to more than a minute.

5. They are usually in motion, either wandering around a space with no apparent pattern or moving straight ahead or up and down.

From here, the descriptions vary widely. Some see the balls move through closed windows or doors. Some watch them follow the line of a metal fence, pipe or wire. Many note that the ball glows with a bright color, from red to orange or green to blue. Few people report that they are aware of a rise in temperature, although they feel cooler when the ball leaves the room or plane. Many people report the smell of sulfur or ozone.

Finally, some of the accounts feature a particularly disturbing event: The ball explodes, spreading catastrophic damage and ending lives.

This is the body of knowledge that was available about ball lightning in 1968, when visitors to Baxter State Park reported to the media that they had observed an uncanny visitation from particularly destructive ball lightning. In just a few moments, they said, the ball took one life, severely injured one other person, and left its angry mark on twenty-two others.

Sudden Death in Chimney Pond Campground

One of the most popular locations in the Baxter backcountry and the gateway to day hikes up Mount Katahdin, Chimney Pond Campground often becomes crowded with hikers and campers in the summer. The camp sits at the bottom of the South Basin, a spectacular spot with a semicircle of 2,000-foot glacier-sculpted granite walls that rise in a cirque around half of the site. Reaching Chimney Pond Camp requires a 3.3-mile hike from the park road and Roaring Brook Campground or a descent from one of Mount Katahdin's peaks, and its campsites fill up early in the evening as hikers prepare for their trek up the mountain the next day, or return from the summit at day's end.

Today advance reservations are required for a place in the ten-person bunkhouse or the use of one of nine lean-tos, and the camp has no tent sites—perhaps because of what happened on the night of August 24, 1968. Back then, campers could bring tents and use what space was available beyond the structures. Scott and Carol Newlin were two such campers—visitors from Philadelphia, they were twenty-seven and twenty-six years old and were clearly worn out when they came off the trail at about 6:15 p.m. and approached Ranger Bernard Gardner at the Chimney Pond station for whatever campsite might be available.

Scott was the kind of star student who grows up to become a model citizen of his community. Well known in his hometown of Coatesville (about forty miles northwest of Philadelphia), Scott strove for leadership of his high school class and was elected vice president, as well as vice president of the elite choir known as the Meistersingers. He served on the student council, played in the band and brass ensemble, and showed aptitude in science early, taking an active role in the chemistry and physics clubs.

Scott's academic success continued in college at Pennsylvania State University. He became a member of both the Phi Kappa Phi and Phi Beta Kappa honor societies in his senior year, and both Scott and his wife, Carol, received their masters' degrees in bacteriology from the University of Iowa. They were working toward their doctorates at the University of Pennsylvania, where Scott had received a fellowship to complete his studies at the Wistar Institute, an academic leader in cancer and infectious disease research. Hilary Koprowski, MD, director of the institute, noted in a letter that Scott was "an investigator in whom we could take great pride. His work and studies here were a reflection of an earnest and upright character and his spirit of willingness was an inspiration to his colleagues."

The Newlins were on the fourth day of a trip that began in Roaring Brook Campground, followed by a hike up the seven-mile Russell Pond Trail to the campground of the same name. They spent the night at Russell Pond, and in the morning they hiked to Big Wassataquoik Lake, where they explored the lake by canoe and returned to Russell Pond Camp for a second night. On their third day in the wild, they continued along the Northwest Basin Trail to the Davis Pond Camp, where they spent the night and completed the Northwest Basin Trail on Saturday. The comparatively short Saddle Trail brought them to Chimney Pond, where after chatting with Gardner, they agreed that they were ready to stop rather than make the three-and-a-half-mile hike over the rocky Chimney Pond Trail back to Roaring Brook that night.

Gardner pointed them to some space at the end of the Dudley Trail beneath a birch tree. He offered them coffee, and they chatted together in the ranger camp before heading off to pitch tent and make camp. By then, heavy clouds had gathered overhead, promising an overcast and potentially soggy night ahead.

"We did camp in our tent, but there wasn't any other option," said Carol Newlin by phone in the winter of 2018 from her home in Colorado, where she is a practicing psychiatrist. "The lean-tos were filled up. The campground was overbooked and overcrowded." A total of 116 campers bedded down in Chimney Pond Campground that night, during one of the last remaining weekends of what had already been a busy summer for Baxter State Park.

The Newlins each carried heavy packs with aluminum frames and all the provisions for another day of hiking. They erected their tent, which had aluminum poles, and unrolled their sleeping bags inside it; instead of pillows, they did what many campers do and made their packs serve double duty, placing them at the open end of their sleeping bag. They made themselves supper in the gathering twilight and turned in by nightfall. "They were in their tent at 9 p.m. when Ranger Gardner made camp check," the park's report noted.

By this time, the ominous clouds signaled heavy rain on its way toward them. "It was calm, but it was very, very interesting," Carol said. "There's a wall of stone, so it's almost a horseshoe-shaped cliff area of stone around there. What was so odd early in the evening was that the clouds were moving in different directions within the horseshoe. It was as if you were seeing two different layers of the air within that horseshoe—left to right, and above it, it was moving almost perpendicular."

Along with the Newlins, the campers that night included members of an adventure camp. These campers had spent the day learning rock climbing and rappelling on various routes on Katahdin, supervised by counselors including Jay Wade and John

Beldin Jr., and junior counselors Winston Theriot and Charlie Jackson, all in their mid-teens. When Jackson heard from Carol Newlin that I was working on this book, he called me to share his own experience.

"We had really nasty tents," Jackson said. "They were army surplus things. Basically, a poncho snapped together with another poncho to make a tent. You had to supply rope to fasten it to a tree. They were as rudimentary as you can imagine."

So when rain began to fall soon after dark, the boys and their counselors had little shelter against what was about to become a massive storm.

"The ranger went down the Roaring Brook Trail to assist a party coming up without lights," the official report said. "At approximately 10:45 p.m., the ranger checked camp again and [the Newlins] were in their tent, apparently sleeping. It was raining quite hard."

By 2 a.m., the dense clouds brought lightning and thunder. The "severe electrical storm," as the report described it, gathered intensity until the violence of a nor'easter-like gale blew into the camp, whipping flaps open and blowing through lean-tos and tents.

"The electricity was everywhere. It was really crazy," said Jackson. "It was a big cirque, and the storm kind of got stuck in there. It actually blew up a rock, big fractures, right next to a tent."

This may have been the "incident" referred to in the report that awakened everyone in the ranger camp at about 4 a.m. It got Ranger Gardner and his family, including his son Judston, out of bed in the middle of the night, when Gardner peered out at the campground and noted a moving ray of light in the area around the Newlins' tent. He pointed it out to Judston, and the young man got dressed and went over to see what was happening.

"Upon his arrival, he found both occupants inside the tent," notes the report. Just a few minutes earlier, however, the force of the wind yanking at the anchors at each corner of the tent had

39

made Scott realize that he needed to retighten and brace the structure against the storm or risk losing what little cover they had. He leapt out into the driving rain, pounding the stakes back into the ground and tightening every loose end he could, anchoring the tent more securely. By the time he returned to shelter, his clothing was drenched. He slipped back into his sleeping bag to get warm.

"He came in just fine," said Carol, "but the fact that he had gone out meant that he was wet." She emphasized this: "I was dry, he was wet."

Carol's vivid memory of this night differs a bit from the official report, but she was hospitalized when the report was compiled and was not interviewed for it. "There were things only I could know," she said.

Judston said in the report that he asked the Newlins to come to the ranger camp so they could be inside for the rest of the night. Scott Newlin declined, saying that they were sheltered and dry enough.

The Gardners went back to bed, but there was little rest in the camp that night. "The storm had, at that point, intensified to an undescribable [sic] fury, both in light and sound," the report said. Thunder crackled and reverberated against the camp's granite walls. The storm parked directly overhead, and the campground was getting the worst of it, a particularly unusual situation—lightning in the park normally focused its energy on the peaks at the top of Mount Katahdin, not down in the Chimney Pond basin.

What they did not know, as Forest Commissioner Austin H. Wilkins told the Associated Press several days later, was that this storm "was of unequalled violence for the Chimney Pond area." The campground saw sudden storms with heavy rains on a regular basis, but this storm remained over the pond for hours and hammered the campground with an intensity that surpassed anything in the park's recorded history.

What happened next can't be pinpointed exactly in the night's frenetic timeline. Witnesses in the campground later told the

Associated Press, "Ball lightning repeatedly flashed into the bowl and circled before going to ground. Large boulders were shattered by the electrical charges and many of the terrified campers felt some of the effects."

The lightning sought and found the ground, its power radiating through every tent and lean-to in the camp. "I remember waking up to this incredible *bam*," Jackson said. "I had burns on my ankles. Campers were groaning and moaning, 'Holy crap, my head aches.' There was an incredible amount of ground current. Almost everyone there at least got a headache out of the deal from being juiced a little bit. A couple of people had burns on their legs, if they had old sleeping bags with metal zippers. The zippers must have heated up. One guy in a lean-to had burns on his legs; I remember watching him bandage them up."

How did the lightning strike and spread through the camp so thoroughly? Later, investigators postulated that it struck the tree under which Scott and Carol pitched their tent, and sent its charge underground through the mighty tree's root system. Its force knocked Scott and Carol unconscious.

The next time Carol awoke, she knew immediately that something was very wrong.

"I looked at Scott, and he was blue," she said, a shade that could not be mistaken for the shadow of their tent's blue fabric. Carol was studying post-graduate biology; she recognized the pallor of cyanosis. "I knew he was dead."

By this time, the storm had finally subsided. Carol got up, and realized right away that something was not right with her own condition, either. "I put one foot in front of the other, over and over," she said, managing to walk slowly, carefully, the hundred yards to the ranger station.

"Mrs. Newlin came knocking at the door of the camp and was admitted by Judston Gardner," the report said. "She told him she was hurt, she didn't know how or what had happened, but she thought her husband was dead."

Bernard and Judston Gardner sprang into action. They left Mrs. Gardner to look after Carol and went to the Newlins' tent, looked in, and quickly began making the rounds of the campground asking if anyone was a doctor. "A man was found in #4 shelter who identified himself as Dr. Reynolds, a physician, and he went to the tent," the park's report noted. He confirmed what Carol had suspected: Scott had been killed by the lightning strike.

Knowing he could do nothing for him, Reynolds turned his attention to Carol.

He determined that Carol had third-degree burns down one entire side of her body. "She was sufficiently aware to give us the first name of herself and her husband, their address and also the name, address and telephone number of her father-in-law," the report notes. "Other than this, she never spoke, except to tell us that she couldn't hear with her right ear. She never mentioned her husband again."

Carol's recollection of those minutes in the ranger camp is punctuated with moments of crystalline clarity. "The clock on the wall in the station stopped at the moment the lightning hit," she told me. "I showed up fifty-five minutes later," at about 6:10 a.m. "I must have looked horrendous, because everybody else was shocked. But I don't think I actually realized what was going on or what had happened to me."

Carol's clothes were shredded along her right side, the side that had been closest to Scott in the sleeping bag. Burn marks and blistered skin followed the line of shredding from her legs all the way up to her face and hair. "The lightning went into my right ear, through my eustachian tube, and burned my mouth," she said. "The eardrum on my right was burned, and it had a little hole in it. So after this I had trouble with high-frequency hearing." Later, a specialist told her that she had experienced two kinds of hearing loss: one from the burn and one from the pressure of the sound wave that coursed through her when the lightning struck.

"I had a pajama top on, a cotton one, that must have been just melted and burned, because a square foot of my chest was burned and into my arm. We had borrowed down sleeping bags, and I heard later that the nylon had burned and the feathers were shredded."

In what must be a characteristic understatement, Carol described the ranger's reaction to her appearance as "surprised." When he asked her for Scott's parents' phone number, she supplied it from memory, a feat that seemed to stun him even further.

"She showed amazing courage and fortitude," he noted in his report.

At 6:15 a.m., Ranger Gardner called the park's Gate #1 to inform them that someone had died at Chimney Pond and that a rescue was required for someone badly injured. A significant obstacle stood between Carol Newlin and medical help: First, she had to survive being carried on a litter for three and a half miles to the Roaring Brook Campground and the park road. The severe burns provided a small blessing, however: shock and nerve damage prevented Carol from feeling pain at this point, a fact that made transporting her out of the park and to a waiting ambulance somewhat easier.

Gardner began to organize a team among the campers currently on site—he needed enough to carry a person on a litter over the challenging, rock-strewn trail. "The ranger came over to talk to the counselors and said, 'We have a rescue to do,'" said Jackson. "Bernie Gardner was well into his sixties. He definitely needed some manpower—there were six or seven of us to carry her out."

Nearby, Camp Invitation to Adventure had a stretcher available, so while Mrs. Gardner helped Carol onto it, wrapped her in blankets, and made her comfortable, Bernard Gardner formed a team that included himself, his son, and willing helpers George Puzzutto, Brian Darke, Kenneth Sharpe, and camp counselors Wade, Beldin, Jackson, and Theriot. Both Invitation to Adventure and another camp at Avalanche Field, Opportunity Farm, supplied some of this assistance. Organizing quickly, the team was in motion and working its way down the trail by 6:55 a.m. "I had always though it was Boy Scouts, but it wasn't—it was these small camping groups," Carol said. "Charlie Jackson told me a few years ago that he remembers how calm everybody was. He remembers that the lightning continued while they carried me down."

Continue it did, Charlie said. "While we were carrying her, a lightning bolt hit a tree, a rotten tree, right next to us—maybe thirty feet off the trail, and it blew up." He added, "That was the most terrifying part of the whole thing."

The men navigated the trail as carefully as they could while trying to make the trip as easy and comfortable as possible for the person on the stretcher. What Carol remembers is a mercifully gentle ride down the rocky path. "I was sort of in and out of it," she said. "When you're carrying a litter like that down a fairly steep path, the people carrying you pass the stretcher—the people carrying the heavier end go to the foot end. I remember them doing that. "

Despite shock and the trauma of losing her husband merely moments before, her memory is solid, Jackson affirmed. "We had to pass the litter down in a lot of places," he said. "When you start passing someone like that, you really take the weight. The next day we could barely move our arms."

Just before they reached the park road, they met a crew of rangers coming up the trail to meet them. They transferred the litter to this fresh group and continued down the trail to the waiting ambulance, where they all helped to get Carol into the vehicle for the twenty-mile ride to the nearest hospital in Millinocket.

"In spite of her husband's death and her own severe burns which covered most of one side of her body, she remained conscious and rational throughout the difficult descent and travel to the hospital," the Associated Press reported. The *Bangor Daily News* noted that Carol "calmly changed her soaked clothing at Roaring Brook before boarding an ambulance for the hospital."

Forest Commissioner Austin H. Wilkins told the AP that he and other officials "can't help marveling at the fortitude of this young woman."

Carol, her voice calm and even, shrugged off this compliment fifty years later. "That's just how I am," she said.

Meanwhile at Chimney Pond Campground, twenty-two other campers found themselves "visibly burned by lightning," according to a note added to the park's report by director Buzz Caverly, with angry red marks and blisters from the electrical storm. "Everyone in the campground was at least jarred by the bolt," he said.

"Most of them, their feet were sticking out of the lean-tos," said Carol. "The doctor was wearing a watch, so he burned where the metal of the watch was."

That's not what happened to Scott, she noted. "It was because my husband was wet, he died of cardiac arrest—that's why he died and I didn't."

Later, when she had the opportunity to think carefully about what had happened, she came to the conclusion that their position at the base of a tree may have been part of the lightning's attraction to their exact spot. "You know how evergreens are and you see a root close to the surface? I assumed a tree had been struck and it came down that surface root toward our camp," she said. "But everyone was near a tall evergreen tree. They were all over the campground."

The Park's Response

While Ranger Gardner and his family saw to the evacuation of Carol Newlin and, later, Scott Newlin's body, the park's front office acted quickly to get the injured woman the help she needed.

Radios had been rendered non-functional by the electrical storm, so Austin H. Wilkins, the park commissioner, received the call about the tragedy from reservation clerk Helen Gifford at about 7:15 a.m. Wilkins notified the members of the Baxter State Park Authority and former governor Percival P. Baxter, and then he made arrangements with the Maine State Police to contact Scott's and Carol's parents as quickly as possible.

Despite the gravity of the situation, Carol remembers some priceless moments. "The police called my parents' house, and my brother, who was eleven, answered the phone," she said. "They asked for my father, who wasn't there, so they didn't leave a message and said they'd call back. They called several times, and my father still wasn't home. Finally the policeman decided to tell my brother why he was calling. He said, 'Carol has been struck by lightning,' but with his Maine accent, it sounded to my brother like he said, 'A cow has been struck by lightning.' So my brother kept asking, 'So why are you calling us?'"

While the police tried to reach Carol's family, Ranger Bill Potter traveled to Nesowadnehunk Field to find Buzz Caverly, whose radio was not working, and tell him what was happening. Caverly drove to pick up Rangers Dave Perkins and Norman Jackson on his way to Roaring Brook—and by the time they arrived at the campground, rangers from all over the park and from the Maine Forest Service had congregated there to help. In all, between twenty-five and thirty-five people were involved in the evacuation of the injured woman and her husband's body.

Caverly and Wilkins went together to the hospital the following day for the task every park director hopes will never be required: a meeting with Scott's parents, Carroll and Helen Newlin, and Carol's father, Dr. David McNary, to try to help them understand what had happened to their children.

Scott's family flew home from Bangor the next day, bringing their son's body with them. Dr. McNary stayed in Millinocket for several days while he made arrangements to bring Carol home to Pennsylvania. During that time, he made several trips to Baxter State Park with Caverly: a flight in a Maine Forest Service plane over the route the young couple had followed on their trek up and around Katahdin, and a hike to Chimney Pond Campground so McNary could see exactly where the lightning strike had so injured his daughter and taken the life of his son-in-law. This gave him "a better mental picture of what had taken place," Caverly noted in the report.

While Dr. McNary worked to understand what had befallen his daughter, others in northern Maine weighed in with their own theories. Dr. Richard Desjardins, who tended to Carol at Millinocket Hospital, suggested that "a contributing factor in the man's death could have been damp clothing." The amount of static electricity in the air could not help but affect others in the campground—and Clayton Gifford of the Maine Forest Service confirmed for the *Bangor Daily News* that all 116 campers at Chimney Pond at the time felt some effects of the massive lightning strike.

After an event like this one, it's no surprise that various experts attempted to provide an explanation for how and why lightning killed one man in the campground and no one else— whether or not they visited the campsite, witnessed the strike, or were there during the storm.

Piscataquis County Deputy Sheriff Joseph A. Bartlett Jr. shared his own theory with reporter Ken Buckley at the *Bangor Daily News*. He said that Scott had pitched his tent next to a small tree, "about eight inches thick and twelve feet tall and it had a root about four inches long pointing directly at the tent—just like a lightning rod." He said that the lightning ran down the tree and "jumped off the finger root, hitting an aluminum rucksack on which one of Newlin's arms was resting." He added, "It blew a hole about four inches in each end of that pup tent," an item not corroborated by the official report.

This story also tells us that Carol "ran through the lightning storm to the Chimney Pond ranger station and pounded on the door." Carol's response to this: "Believe me, I didn't run anywhere. I moved very, very slowly, one foot in front of the other."

The newspaper also sought the opinion of Frank H. Todd, a physics professor at the University of Maine, who said that when lightning strikes and reaches the ground, it is "very unusual" for it to jump back up into metal. "Theoretically, if the tent poles were in deep earth, the strike should have been carried down into the earth," the paper noted. "Citing aluminum as a good lightning conductor, Todd said that metal conductors should be well grounded into the deep damp earth and people should make sure that connections are good."

Carol dismissed the theory that aluminum caused the strike. "I kept my H-frame backpack, which had very few pockmarks— less than the size of a pencil eraser," she said. "I think wetness was the principal factor, like warnings not to have electric gadgets in the bathtub."

In the end, when death is caused by a phenomenon that lasts less than a second, determining exactly what happened can become a futile exercise. Commissioner Wilkins said that since the accident was obviously an act of nature, no inquiry beyond the written report would be required to investigate Scott Newlin's death.

Caverly added his own observations at the end of the report. "As I have reviewed this accident many times in the past few weeks, I have asked myself what steps could have been taken to prevent such a tragedy," he wrote. "I have finally come to the conclusion that it was just a freak of Nature. No one was to blame, and nothing can be done to prevent this from happening again. All we can do is accept it and deal with it to [the] best of our ability."

Earlier in the report, however, he did make one significant suggestion: "It is my personal recommendation that no tenting on the ground be allowed at Chimney Pond."

Caverly's advice became a hard-and-fast rule. Today tent camping is not permitted at Chimney Pond Campground.

A Long Path to Recovery

Three days after the lightning strike, the Associated Press reported that Carol Newlin was "in good condition in a Millinocket hospital but will need several months of treatment before her burns are healed."

Carol's actual recovery time stretched well beyond her hospital stay. Five years would pass before she finally felt like the experience had come to an end.

She spent the first ten days after the lightning strike in Millinocket Hospital under the care of Dr. Desjardins. Carol did not engage in any of the speculation that swirled around what the papers were calling Scott's "electrocution." Instead, she focused as best she could on her own recovery in the wake of the loss of her husband, staying away from the media and resting in a hospital far from her home.

"The 1968 Democratic Convention was going on, where they had all the riots," she recalled. "I don't remember a lot about that time, because they didn't do any procedures, and I was pretty well blistered. But I remember seeing those riots on TV."

From Millinocket, Carol flew with her father in a small, private ambulance plane provided by the New England Flyers Air Service to Clearfield, Pennsylvania, to refuel, and then on to Allegheny Airport—making a tricky manual landing when the plane's radio stopped working. At South Side Hospital in Pittsburgh on the Monongahela River, doctors supervised her care. "It was right across from the J&M Steel Company, and [my doctor] had treated a lot of burns from the steel mill," Carol said. "I was there until the week after Thanksgiving," a total of three months. Here she had six procedures: one debridement surgery to remove all the damaged skin, and then five skin grafts.

"Right before Christmas, I came out and went back to my apartment in Philadelphia for a visit," she said. "I really couldn't speak much at that time. I had a lot of learning and memory things, an inability to express things."

Carol and Scott were both graduate students at the University of Pennsylvania. After her ordeal in Maine and her semester-long hospital stay, her department not only welcomed her back, but they took her under their wing and gave her the support she needed to continue her studies and earn her doctorate in immunology. "My PhD advisor arranged for a visiting foreign student to stay in my apartment," she said. "She was a lab tech from Israel. The fact that I had a roommate with very limited English—it was like learning language again for me. She and I were roommates for three years."

As she regained her ability to express herself, Carol completed her PhD in 1971, three years after the accident, and received her degree in 1972. She remained at the university for a fellowship in biochemistry, and then went on to medical school in 1974. "For me, the year when I was accepted into medical school was when it became normal again," she said. She completed her medical degree in 1979 and followed it with a residency in psychiatry.

Fifty years after the lightning strike, she can look back with quiet objectivity. "I feel like it's more interesting to other people than it is to me," she said.

And what of Charlie Jackson? The fourteen-year-old who helped carry Carol out of the backcountry recalls suffering from something like post-traumatic stress disorder for some time after the incident, but that didn't dampen his love of the outdoors. "I was afraid of the dark, afraid of the stars; it was really weird," he said. "At fourteen, I really knew that people do die and bad things happen. It gave me a perspective of what is scary and what isn't."

He indulged his passion for rock climbing in parks across the country, climbing Yosemite National Park's El Capitan at seventeen and even serving on the Yosemite search-and-rescue team for several summers in the early 1970s. When he was ready to consider a career, he became an arborist and tree surgeon.

"Six weeks before I got married, I fell out of a tree, broke my back, and slipped a vertebra," he said. This accident and the responsibilities of marriage put an end to his interest in high-risk rock climbing and other such pursuits, and after a crazy-quilt career in a number of professions, he chose home construction as his main focus. Now officially retired, he's still building houses when a project catches his fancy.

His son's interest led Charlie to get back in touch with Carol in 2008. "He'd been doing some screenwriting, and was talking about going to Hollywood, and he said to me, 'I need a story.' So I told him this story, and then I realized I never knew what happened to Carol, or even if she survived. So I looked her up. It made it all worthwhile for me, knowing that she lived."

The Shape of Lightning

Despite witnesses' accounts of the incident in the media, the park's official report of the August night in 1968 does not attribute the damage and injuries to ball lightning. Whether they dismissed the eyewitnesses' descriptions as hokum, or they decided to go with more conventional science on the matter, the results were the same: Scott Newlin was dead, his wife was severely injured, twenty-two other people were burned, and the most violent storm in Chimney Pond Campground's history had left an indelible mark in the park's records.

Oddly enough, the first true breakthrough in our understanding of ball lightning came very recently—in August 2017, from researchers at Zhenjiang University in Hangzhou, China.

These scientists theorize that ball lightning is the result of microwaves trapped inside a plasma bubble. They suggest that when a bolt of lightning touches the ground, it can produce an electron bunch that causes "intense microwave radiation." This creates plasma and forms a bubble, and the microwave radiation becomes trapped inside. The microwaves continue to generate plasma, maintaining the intense light until the radiation begins to dissipate. If the microwaves remain within the plasma bubble during this process, the ball simply disappears. If they leak out of the bubble, however, the ball can explode.

I'll spare you the lengthy scientific explanation that contains words like "monoenergetic & MeV electron bunch" and "coherent transition radiation," but if their theory is correct, these researchers may be able to create ball lightning in a laboratory, allowing further study under controlled conditions. One day, it may be possible to tell whether the force of this natural phenomenon could have been at work in Baxter State Park so many decades ago.

Decades Later: Strike Near Pamola Peak

Two other lightning strikes on Mount Katahdin have resulted in fatalities. One of these singled out a thirteen-year-old Boy Scout, just as he reached Pamola Peak with nine other scouts and two adult leaders.

The troop traveled to Maine from Manhasset, a town on Long Island, New York, for a multi-day backpacking trip. They had gained considerable experience hiking in wilderness areas from 1987 to 1990, so they were properly prepared to set out for Pamola Peak on Monday, August 27, 1990. The day looked like a fine one for their hike, with a 30 percent chance of rain late in the day. No angry clouds threatened, however, so when they reached Baxter Peak and looked out over Knife Edge, they were confident that they could cross it safely.

As these young hikers and their leaders knew, every mountain hike above the tree line requires a measure of caution, as weather can change in the space of a few minutes. The scouts and their leaders were nearly all the way across the 1.1-mile section of exposed trail and within a few minutes' reach of Pamola Peak at about 4 p.m., when gathering clouds turned dark and burst open right over their heads. Heavy rain pelted the trail, and lightning and thunder erupted around them just a few feet past the end of Knife Edge. Any shelter from forest canopy or manmade structure was half an hour ahead of them at best. Soaked but hopeful that the storm would blow past them as quickly as it had come, they plodded on through driving rain and wind, continuing to approach one of the highest points in the state of Maine.

Katahdin's peaks attract lightning the way wool socks attract cockleburs. The mountain's high rock faces bear the scars of countless strikes, as Percival P. Baxter himself described in a speech to the 1921 annual meeting of the Maine Sportsmen's Fish and Game Association.

The climb to Pamola Peak by a rough trail through stunted pine, over great granite boulders that lie spilled in endless drifts on the side of the Mountain, up the steep slope to the summit, down into the "Chimney" where the rush of air threatens to tear one's feeble grasp from the cliffs to which one clings, and then across the treacherous "Knife Edge" to Mountain peak, is both difficult and dangerous. . . . On every hand were countless marks of the lightning's work, which looked like the spattering of lead from bullets that had struck upon the stone leaving a grayish film surrounded by shattered rock. Lightning has bombarded this Mountain top for ages, but Katahdin, unconquered and unafraid, still holds aloft its noble head.

Perhaps the boys and their leaders held back from the peak itself through the storm, as the American Alpine Club's accident report notes that they were "within 100 meters of Pamola Peak" when the worst of the storm reached them. Nearing the end of Knife Edge, however, they were completely exposed to the elements—and when lightning forked its way down from the clouds to the mountain, it found two fourteen-year-olds, David Passalacqua and Fred Ulrich, in its path.

The bolt scorched Ulrich's head, neck, and leg as it sliced between the boys and made contact with the granite ridgeline, sending a jolt of electrical power through all of the hikers. In less than a second, it was gone . . . and with it went Passalacqua's life.

Minutes later, the storm had passed, and the boys and their leaders faced a new challenge: getting medical help for the injured boy, securing Passalacqua's body for evacuation, and bringing the rest of the troop home safely. They rose to the occasion and shepherded the boys back down the mountain without further incident, notifying the ranger at Chimney Pond Campground of the boy whose body waited near Pamola Peak.

Scoutmaster Steve Sassi remained with Ulrich overnight in the ranger's cabin at Chimney Pond Camp, while more rainstorms raged around them. At first light on Tuesday, a helicopter arrived to bring them off the mountain to Millinocket Regional Hospital, where young Fred received trauma care until he could be transferred to the pediatric intensive care unit at Eastern Maine Medical Center. A second helicopter traveled to the spot below Pamola Peak where the scoutmasters had secured Passalacqua's body, and a rescue team brought the boy's remains down from the mountain.

Death at Katahdin Stream

Just one other visitor perished as the result of a lightning strike on Mount Katahdin, and this one also met an untimely end while in camp.

On August 25, 2007, Evans and Emmett Huber of Peaks Island, Maine, and their mother, Lois Tiedeken, selected a campsite in Katahdin Stream Campground that happened to be close to a tree. The camp is a particularly popular spot because of its position at the beginning of the Hunt Trail, which traces the last few miles of the Appalachian Trail on its way to its terminus at the Katahdin summit.

During the night, a thunderstorm swept through the camp, dumping rain and bringing thunder that echoed against the mountainside. In a crescendo of crackling energy, a lightning bolt hit the tree nearest to the Hubers' campsite, deflected into the camp, and struck both the Hubers.

Twenty-four-year-old Evans died instantly. "Baxter State Park staff responded to the scene and attempted to revive the elder Huber but were unsuccessful," the *Burlington Free Press* reported two days later. Rescuers acted quickly to assess eighteen-year-old Emmett's wounds, and arranged for transportation to bring him to Millinocket Regional Hospital. He was treated for first- and second-degree burns on his feet. Remarkably, their mother escaped without physical injury.

This was the last death of any kind in Baxter State Park for ten years. Not until 2017 would another visitor meet a bad end in the park, and his story comes at the end of chapter 12.

CHAPTER 4

The Shortcut, the Hurricane, and the Search

OF ALL THE CAUTIONARY TALES OF PEOPLE WHO HAVE LOST their lives in parks across the country, none are sadder than those that include the loss of people who attempted to rescue them. This is one of those stories, an epic drama in which a ranger trekked into the rugged backcountry alone in the middle of a blizzard, because he could not rest knowing that someone needed his help. For years afterward, this episode became known as the Mount Katahdin Tragedy—but some good came of it as well: a complete overhaul of Baxter State Park's search-and-rescue operations, with procedures and protocols that save many, many more lives than they sacrifice.

On a balmy October Saturday in 1963, Mrs. Margaret Ivusic, a fifty-two-year-old Boston resident, and her friend, Mrs. Helen Mower of Concord, Massachusetts, arrived at Roaring Brook Campground. The sun was already dipping toward the western horizon as they drove up to the ranger station, where Ranger Ralph Heath greeted them. He handed them a copy of the park's rules and regulations, and they chatted about the women's hiking plans. Margaret and Helen intended to hike to the top of Mount Katahdin from Chimney Pond, but they knew this would require an early-morning start from the backcountry campground. They decided to find accommodations outside of the park for Saturday evening, and then hike into Chimney Pond from Roaring Brook first thing Sunday morning.

Margaret and Helen had seen their share of trails in recent years. Helen Mower had been hiking since she was a child, taking on a number of the tallest mountains in New England and enjoying many a woodland trail. Margaret Ivusic had taken up hiking in the last two or three years to spend time with her friend, but she had accumulated considerable experience in an effort to keep up with the more adept Mrs. Mower. They knew that weather could be changeable without warning on the region's highest peaks, so they carried additional clothing, food, and other supplies to ensure their own safety in the backcountry. Neither woman, however, expected that this hike would be any more hazardous than any of the challenging treks they had completed before.

The pleasantly warm temperatures continued on Sunday, so the hiking partners loaded up their packs, parked their car at Roaring Brook, and made their way up the trail to Chimney Pond. There they once again ran into Heath, who assigned them a lean-to, and they met Ranger Rodney Sargent as well. They all discussed the various routes up Katahdin and which were the best match for the hikers' skills. The women settled into their lean-to, made supper, and bedded down for the night.

Before 8 o'clock Monday morning, October 28, the two women exchanged pleasantries with the rangers once again and set out for the Cathedral Trail. At the same time, Heath and Sargent began hiking up the Dudley Trail to reach the Helon Taylor Trail, where they had a full day of trail work planned.

Margaret and Helen made their way up the Cathedral Trail to Baxter Peak, reaching this summit at about 1:30 p.m. "Here they stopped for lunch, took some pictures and rested for quite some time," the official report notes. When they resumed their hike, they decided to venture out onto the Knife Edge Trail, "although they were not sure whether they would continue along that trail and return to camp or retrace their steps and return by way of the Saddle Trail," Helen told the Baxter State Park Authority later.

Like many pairs or groups of hikers who know one another well, Margaret and Helen did not always walk side by side or follow one another closely on trails. "It was not uncommon for one or the other of [us] to walk on ahead of the other on these hikes," Helen explained to the park authorities. Once they were on Knife Edge, Margaret got some distance ahead of Helen, enough so that Helen lost sight of her for ten or fifteen minutes. Then Margaret called back to Helen that she had found a shortcut to Chimney Pond, leading down from Knife Edge, and that she had started down that way.

"I think this is the best way to go," Margaret told Helen.

Helen looked ahead of the sound of Margaret's voice, and admitted that the route did look like a short and easier way. She could see the pond and the camp from there, and it appeared that the route might be a good option. Leaving the marked trail, however, struck her as ill-advised. She told Margaret that she did not think the shortcut was a good idea.

At this point, Helen could not see Margaret, but each of the women attempted to hammer her point home. "We are both determined women," Helen told the board of inquiry weeks later. Finally, with neither of them giving an inch, they decided that each would go her own way and they would meet back at the campground.

As she hiked along Knife Edge, Helen called out to Margaret repeatedly to try to maintain voice contact with her. Margaret did not respond, so Helen continued until she came to the top of Chimney Trail. Here the sign at the top of the trail alarmed her. It cautioned that only experienced climbers carrying ropes should attempt to go down that way. Helen realized that her friend had taken this route, and she may have found herself overwhelmed by the challenge.

Helen called down the trail to see if Margaret was indeed on it. This time Margaret responded that she was "on the wall and could not move up or down."

She was not injured, but she did not have the gear or experience to make her way back to camp.

Helen told Margaret to stay where she was, and that she would go back to Chimney Pond as quickly as she could to get help.

"I'll see you tomorrow, I hope," Margaret said to her.

Helen took the Dudley Trail to Chimney Pond Camp and arrived at about 6:40 p.m., but it was already dark and she found no rangers on site. She walked to the edge of Chimney Pond and shouted up to where she believed Margaret remained stranded. Sure enough, Margaret called back to her, and they remained in voice communication through the evening as Helen moved back and forth between the pond and her campsite, building a fire in front of her lean-to and leaving it periodically to keep talking to Margaret.

At 8:15 p.m., Ralph Heath returned to Chimney Pond Camp. Helen approached him immediately and told him about Margaret and her precarious situation on the Chimney Trail. "It was obvious that Heath had worked hard that day and he seemed extremely tired," she told the authorities. She urged him to rest before attempting a rescue, and Heath walked to Chimney Pond and called up to Margaret to assess her condition. Apparently assured that she was not hurt and in no immediate danger, he told Margaret to stay put, and that he would be up to help her down the trail at first light.

Margaret had "lots of clothes" with her, Helen told the authorities later, "and in addition, she had a wool shirt and an arctic jacket that was tied around her waist." She was well prepared to wait out a chilly night if necessary.

Heath and Mrs. Mower settled into the ranger camp and had some soup for supper, and he made his usual evening call to

Park Supervisor Helon Taylor, during which he informed him that Margaret Ivusic was stranded on the mountain. Heath and Taylor agreed that her situation was not "serious," and Helen went off to bed in her lean-to while Heath attempted to get some rest in his cabin.

That night, the weather changed.

For the last ten days, a tropical cyclone had hovered off the east coast of the United States, teasing its way back and forth between the Bahamas, Florida, and North Carolina. Suddenly it turned northward and headed for the coast of New England. As it crossed into the northeastern United States, Hurricane Ginny had become an extratropical cyclone with winds of up to 110 miles per hour.

Ginny's passage triggered a snowstorm the likes of which are rarely seen in October, even in northern Maine. The influx of cold air caused the first snowfall of the season, beginning just before midnight on Monday, October 28, when Ranger Heath heard a storm door banging and realized that the weather was about to take a significant turn for the worse.

Heath arose and left his cabin, borrowed the rucksack Margaret had left in camp, and filled it with food, her parka, sleeping bag, extra clothing, and a piton and eighty feet of rope. He started out up the Dudley Trail.

Several hours later, at about 4 a.m. on Tuesday, October 29, Heath returned to camp. He told Helen that he had determined Margaret's location and had attempted to reach her by going down off of Knife Edge for some distance, the last forty feet of it on a rope. He had spoken with Margaret, but he could not reach her without more rope, so he promised her that he would return after it was light with additional help.

Heath ate a hurried breakfast and called Park Supervisor Taylor, putting in his request for assistance. He explained that he believed she was located near "the waterfall," a well-known landmark west of the Chimney Trail, and "the sooner we get her off, the better." By this time a driving wind had come up in advance of Hurricane Ginny's full arrival, and icy rain pelted the camp. Taylor dispatched Sargent and Ranger Owen Grant to Chimney Pond to assist, but Heath's concern for Margaret overrode his better judgment. He decided not to wait for additional help to arrive and set out once again on his own at 6:10 a.m. He told Helen that he intended to "go around to the right of Chimney Pond and approach the waterfall from below."

As he started down the trail, Helen heard the radio in the ranger cabin crackle and Ranger Sargent's voice say that he was on his way to the camp. Helen ran after Heath and shouted this message to him.

"Fine, thank you," Heath shouted back.

That was the last anyone heard from Ranger Ralph Heath.

Later, Ranger Sargent told the Baxter State Park Authority panel of inquiry that Heath had been up through the ravine near the waterfall without ropes on a number of occasions. In good weather, this would have been a fairly routine climb for the thirty-seven-year-old ranger. This particular day, however, brought weather so uncharacteristic of this time of year that Heath could not possibly have predicted the hazards ahead.

"The weather was such you couldn't breathe," Sargent told author Phyllis Austin in her book, *Wilderness Partners*. "The force of the wind took your breath away. Above tree line your clothes froze. I knew if Ralph was on the headwall there was no hope."

Meanwhile, Taylor notified Forest Warden Clayton Gifford in Millinocket and Elmer Knowlton, Fisheries and Game Warden, of the search effort. People began to arrive at Chimney Pond: Sargent got there from his home camp at Abol at about 7:45 a.m. and Warden Grant was there by 8:05. By then, two inches of snow had already accumulated, and snowfall picked up its pace through the morning. Sargent talked with Helen Mower and got his bearings, snowshoeing to the base of the Chimney and calling upward to try to determine where Heath and Mrs. Ivusic might be. Twenty minutes of shouting generated no response.

As much as eight inches of snow had fallen by the time Sargent returned. Conditions worsened as the day went on, preventing Knowlton and Taylor from traversing the park in a four-wheel drive vehicle with chains on its wheels. It was nightfall on Tuesday before they reached Roaring Brook, and from there Knowlton hiked into Chimney Pond through deep snow and up the Dudley Trail, calling and using his flashlight to alert Ralph and Margaret to his presence. No one responded. Knowlton returned to camp and struck out again, following the Chimney Pond Trail the way they believed that Heath had gone, but with the heavy snowfall, there were no tracks to follow and no signs of human activity,

Wednesday morning, October 30, dawned with sleet and rain falling on top of two feet of new snow. Gale-force winds made blowing and drifting snow a major obstacle to the continued search, which now included Warden David Priest and several additional wardens he'd brought into Roaring Brook that morning. As they loaded packs to head up the trail to Chimney Pond, two woodsmen met them on their return trip. They said that the deep snow and whiteout conditions had made it impossible for them to reach the backcountry camp. Still, Priest and the wardens started up the trail and on the way met Ranger Sargent, who led them in the rest of the way to Chimney Pond. Priest decided to set up a search headquarters and coordinate the effort from Roaring Brook.

By this time wardens and climbers were arriving from throughout the state to assist in the search for the missing ranger and hiker. As many as thirty-five people were gathered at any one time, Priest told the authorities, but "weather conditions were a tremendous factor. You can't visualize the wind and snow. Visibility was zero, and that's putting it mildly."

The blizzard continued through Thursday, October 31. For a short time on Friday, November 1, the weather broke and cleared

... and then the rain began. Two days of rain turned the trails into sluices of water, ice, and mud. Even in these conditions, however, a team of climbers from the University of Maine put in the best effort they could to scale Knife Edge, Baxter Peak, and Pamola Peak, but they were forced back again and again by the winds and blowing snow. Finally on Friday, November 1, they reached the Cathedral Trail and had the opportunity to scan the walls below with binoculars, but they saw no flash of color that might indicate a person's clothing.

On Thursday night, Priest sat down with Maynard Marsh, chief of the Maine Warden Service, to talk through a plan of action once the weather broke. The greatest need, Priest told Marsh, was for "experienced rock men," people who knew how to conduct large-scale searches in the roughest terrain. Marsh suggested that he get in touch with William Putnam, a mountain search-and-rescue professional in Springfield, Massachusetts. It took one phone call to engage Putnam, and he and another climber flew up to Maine on Friday, November 1. At the same time, Commissioner Austin H. Wilkins heard from a man in Vermont that a team of Vermont State Troopers was standing by to assist in the search, and they arrived on a National Guard C-47 plane on Friday as well.

The questions Putnam asked on his arrival brought to light the deficiencies in the search effort up to that point. No log had been kept on what areas had been searched and what methods had been used to do so. The effort lacked a specific director, so no one served as the clearinghouse for all information or coordinator of personnel. The scattershot approach may not have been the only reason for the searchers' lack of success to date, but it certainly did not help. Putnam began to work closely with the park supervisors to bring organization and focus to the flagging effort, breaking the searchers into groups on Saturday morning, November 2, to make as thorough a sweep of the area as possible.

One group headed up the Dudley Trail in hopes of discovering that Heath had taken that route after all, and that he had sought shelter under an overhang or in a depression in the rock. Other groups headed upward to Pamola Peak, with the goal of retracing Margaret's steps down the Chimney or another ravine to the west of the landmark. When the groups heading upward reached the top of Chimney, however, Putnam realized that the weather made it virtually impossible to proceed safely. The fifth day of snow, wind, and sleet had encased the trail in a combination of hard, dry, windblown snow and wet slush, and he understood with the clarity of an impartial observer that no one could have survived in this "ferocious" storm for five days. In fact, he became certain that the storm had taken Margaret's and Ranger Heath's lives on Tuesday, the first day of the blizzard. "It's the wind that kills you," he said during the inquiry.

Still, it took two more days before the would-be rescuers fully accepted that the search must come to an end. Resigning themselves to the inevitable, the climbers from Vermont and Massachusetts left for home on Sunday. On Monday, November 4, eight days after Margaret Ivusic and Ralph Heath had disappeared in the storm, Commissioners Ronald T. Speers and Wilkins and Warden Priest came to agreement that the search was closed. They notified Governor Reed that the hiker and the ranger had been lost.

"You continued the search far longer than any mountaineer would have considered necessary under the prevailing conditions," Putnam told them later. He then reported the shortcomings of the search effort to the American Alpine Club in their annual publication of the year's accident reports: "There was confusion and delay at all stages of this operation in calling for sufficient competent help to get the job done properly. The severity of the storm on Tuesday, October 29, was such that no amount of competent help could have arrived in time to do any good even had they been called at first radio contact. Subsequent hearings have pointed out the need to develop sounder procedures in Maine in order to eliminate confusion and delay in the future, and the need for central control of operations."

The initial search ended without success, but the incident remained at the forefront of the minds of park leaders as the November blizzard finally abated. Winter set in as it always does on Mount Katahdin, and staff members began to plan for the day in April when they would return to the trails to find Margaret's and Heath's remains.

"During that winter, wardens Donald Gray and Roger Spaulding were sent to New York State to receive some training in ice climbing, in anticipation of the chore that lay ahead come spring," wrote Warden Eric Wight in his book, *Life and Death in the North Woods*. Austin's book reports that Ranger Sargent went for this training as well, which took place in New Paltz, New York—most likely in the Shawangunk Mountains, an area legendary for its rock formations. "Later that winter, they were on the mountain instructing other wardens in the techniques they had learned. The nucleus of our eventual rescue team had taken shape."

Snow finally began to melt in April. Warden Knowlton and another warden, Charlie Merrill, climbed to Pamola Peak and scanned the slopes below with binoculars until Knowlton spotted something manmade far below him. A rope hung over a rock ledge—the first sign that Heath had managed to reach and attempted to rescue Margaret Ivusic six months earlier.

Knowlton and Merrill contacted the search teams. "They began the arduous task of locating the bodies, freeing them from their icy tombs, and transporting them off the mountain," Wight said. The five-man team moved into Chimney Pond Camp on Tuesday, April 28, with plans to make an early start up the still-icy trail on Wednesday morning.

On Wednesday, April 29, exactly six months after she disappeared, the recovery team found Margaret Ivusic near the lower end of the rope, about a third of the way down from Pamola Peak and 1,600 feet up from Chimney Pond. She had perished in a depression in the rock, where Heath may have moved her to get her out of the wind until rescuers arrived. Heath had done his best to protect her from the elements, providing a sleeping bag and covering her with two bright red raincoats.

It had taken all day just to locate Margaret, so by the time the team could consider what freeing her body from the ice would entail, it was late in the afternoon. They made their way down the cliffs, a six-hour descent that required all of their newly acquired ice-climbing skills. "The climbers reported to park headquarters that the trail had to be improved before it would be safe to carry the body down," the Associated Press reported later that day.

The search team returned the following day to begin chopping away the ice that held her body like a sarcophagus—and when chopping proved ineffective, the team brought in chemical salt to break up the ice, reports author Peter W. Kick in his book, *Desperate Steps: Life, Death and Choices Made in the Mountains of the Northeast.* Even with this assistance, the recovery team put in three days of effort to release her body. They transported it to Knife Edge on a litter and carried the litter to Thoreau Spring, where she was lifted out by air.

To the searchers' chagrin, they found no sign of Ralph Heath. Two weeks later, however, on May 16, enough snow had melted to reveal Heath's body about four hundred feet from Margaret Ivusic. The team recovered the body and brought it to a position where it could be airlifted out by helicopter.

The team guessed that Heath had fallen and injured himself in the blizzard, but this turned out not to be the case. "An autopsy indicated that Heath died of exposure after being caught in the blizzard last October," the Associated Press reported. "There was no direct evidence of injury, as might have been suffered in a fall, the autopsy disclosed."

The team brought Heath's body down from the mountain on Sunday, May 17, closing a grim chapter in the history of Mount Katahdin and Baxter State Park. Park Director Buzz Caverly was "torn apart emotionally," Austin's book tells us. "Heath was not only a special friend; Buzz knew it would have been him on the mountain with Ivusic if he hadn't traded days off with Heath. Buzz made a promise to himself that he would never let Heath's ultimate sacrifice be forgotten over time. He became loyal to the lost ranger's memory in word and deed for the rest of his career."

Some good did come of these tragic events, however: Maine's State Fish and Game Department now had a trained mountain rescue team, a formal chain of command for emergency situations, and procedures in place to conduct large-scale search-and-rescue operations, even in treacherous conditions. They also acquired appropriate equipment and proper clothing for winter searches. "In Buzz's mind, Heath's death also underscored the need for the right clothing and best equipment for rescues," Austin wrote. "When Heath went out to look for Ivusic, he was wearing cotton clothes, not wool, and thus was unprotected from the severe cold and wet weather he encountered. 'I always thought that Ralph Heath went further than the rest of us would have,' says Buzz. 'He had courage . . . he certainly was not thinking of himself.'"

The insights gathered from the difficult search of 1963 meant that the vast majority of future searches would result in rescues, a good-news ending to one of the park's saddest stories.

Meanwhile, a Mysterious Disappearance

Even as the ice-climbing rescue team recovered Ralph Heath's body from Katahdin, another search had begun in and around Roaring Brook Campground for a man who had simply vanished.

Roger Hildreth, a fifty-four-year-old real-estate broker from Lowell, Massachusetts, left Lowell on May 6, 1964, on a road trip with his friend, forty-six-year-old Arthur L. Plourde. They planned to drive up to Quebec, Hildreth told his parents—one of whom was Charles S. Hildreth, who was well known in the Lowell area as the town clerk of nearby Westford for five decades—and he would return home on May 17.

Roger Hildreth called his folks on May 6 from the St. Regis Hotel in Portsmouth, New Hampshire. Millinocket residents later told police that they had seen Hildreth and Plourde the next evening, together at a snack bar in town at about midnight. From there, the two men drove into Baxter State Park and arrived in the Roaring Brook Campground at about 2 a.m., where they stopped for the night. They slept in Hildreth's station wagon until about 5 a.m., when Hildreth left the car, took a bag of food with him, and went off "to take a look at the sunrise," Plourde said later. He was dressed in light clothing and wore street shoes, leaving him ill-equipped for the chilly spring morning in Maine's north woods.

Hildreth never returned to the car. After waiting for him for a time and trying to find him on his own, Plourde went to the cabin of Ranger James Smith at Roaring Brook and reported Hildreth missing.

Here's where the story gets weird.

Plourde also talked to Ranger Laurel Bouchard, who approached his white station wagon in the Roaring Brook parking area. "As he approached it, a man stepped out to meet him—a man, Bouchard said, with a face battered from scores of brawls, skinned knuckles and a broken wrist watch," *Boston Globe* reporter Jerome Sullivan wrote. "'I'm worried about my friend,' he said. 'He ought to be back by now. He went up the trail to see if he could find where the body of that woman from Boston is,'" apparently referring to Margaret Ivusic, whose body had been found several weeks earlier.

Smith (or possibly Bouchard, as accounts mention both rangers) immediately took to the trail and walked more than three miles to the snow line on Mount Katahdin. The ranger saw no trace of the missing man—no footprints, food wrappers, scraps, or anything that would indicate that Hildreth had passed this way.

"A man couldn't possibly have walked up there that day without leaving tracks," Bouchard told the *Boston Globe*. In mid-spring, the Chimney Pond Trail's surface yielded easily to the weight of a man, so anyone passing would leave tracks in the earth. Farther up the trail's vertical slope, a hiker would leave distinct tracks in the snow. "At times I was down on all fours," looking for any sign of the missing man, Bouchard added.

"Plourde told me that he and Hildreth had bought food in Millinocket the night before," the ranger continued. "He said they had been on a trip together, that he had been chauffeuring for Hildreth and they had been traveling for a week." Their trip included visits to Quebec and Vermont, Plourde told him. The length of the trip he described, however, differed from the actual time the men had been on the road, as far as rangers and police could determine.

Now the park mobilized its search-and-rescue operation, using twenty-five men including game wardens, forest rangers, Maine State Police, park officials, and "experienced mountain men" to canvass the area on the ground and from the air, using two Fish and Game Department planes. Maine State Police brought bloodhounds to the scene and attempted to follow Hildreth's scent, but the dogs "led handlers on inconclusive trails to a pond and a bog," the *Boston Globe* reported. Pilot Andy Stinson took an observer on Tuesday, May 12, and covered the South Turner–Mount Katahdin Lake area, but saw nothing that would indicate Hildreth was or had ever been in the area.

After five days of searching, Warden Supervisor David Priest told the media that their efforts had borne no fruit. He called Hildreth's total disappearance "extremely unusual," and admitted that he did not expect him to be found at all, much less alive. "There are no clues, no trails . . . nothing," he told the *Globe*.

Baxter State Park Superintendent Helon Taylor added: "There isn't even proof that Hildreth is in the woods."

The Fish and Game Department officially ended its search on May 13, as baffled as they were when Hildreth's disappearance was first reported. "I believe we have now done all we can," Chief Warden Maynard F. Marsh told the media in Augusta. Priest intended to send a search party up Mount Katahdin, the one area that had not been searched, but that would be the last step the park would take to locate the missing man.

The lack of any shred of a trail pointed to the possibility of foul play, leading park authorities to welcome a police investigation. Hildreth, after all, was a well-to-do man who might have had valuables on him when he disappeared. The police turned the case over to the Criminal Investigation Bureau, which assigned Detective Carl Buchanan of Orono to lead the effort to determine if Hildreth had been kidnapped—or perhaps even murdered.

The police in Hildreth's hometown of Lowell became involved as well, especially when they began to receive "several mysterious phone calls" with potential leads to the missing man's whereabouts. One such call suggested that they search a camp some distance from the park, at Long Pond in Pelham, New Hampshire—and the female caller also phoned Hildreth's wife with the same information. Police proceeded to the camp and searched it thoroughly, but nothing there pointed to Hildreth or to any kind of unusual activity, criminal or otherwise.

Meanwhile, things were not going well for Arthur Plourde, Hildreth's traveling companion. On Wednesday night, May 20, about two weeks after Hildreth's disappearance, Lowell police arrested Plourde for public drunkenness, bringing him into the station for booking and further questioning about his friend's case. Captain Richard Cullen went over the entire episode with Plourde again from the beginning, and reported, "He replied to his questions without hesitation and that he practically repeated the answers he had given previously to Maine and Lowell officials."

In the midst of this questioning, however, Cullen heard from Detective Ferdinand Giobri of the Portland Criminal Bureau about a strange incident that had taken place the day before Hildreth disappeared. The *Boston Globe* described this in detail:

Cullen said the incident involved a ferry trip by Hildreth to Peaks Island in Portland Harbor. He said police investigated a story told by both Plourde and Hildreth that just as the vessel was pulling out, Hildreth threw some money over the ferry's side to Plourde on the dock, but the wind scattered it and some bills were grabbed by others.

Plourde reportedly argued with these people, bringing on police intervention. Police with Plourde waited until Hildreth returned aboard the ferry and confirmed that the money was Hildreth's.

Hildreth always carried a lot of cash with him, Plourde apparently confirmed. Ranger Bouchard noted this: "My wife went out to the station wagon to give Plourde a cup of coffee and saw a lot of cash in the car. She said there was a checkbook there on the seat and there was cash stuffed in that." Indeed, the facts bore this out: On May 6, the day Hildreth and Plourde left on their trip, Hildreth visited his bank in Lowell and withdrew $2,300 from his savings account.

With the new details of this incident on the table and Plourde already in custody, Captain Cullen asked Plourde to take a lie-detector test. Plourde readily agreed, and he went with Detective Giobri to Portland to undergo the test. The results were negative: Plourde was telling the truth that he was not involved in any foul play that led to Hildreth's disappearance. Cullen told the media that he was convinced that Plourde "had nothing to do with the disappearance."

Now more strange details began to emerge. Sullivan at the *Globe* delved into Hildreth's medical history—something the media could do back in 1964, decades before passage of the patient privacy law known as HIPAA—and discovered that Hildreth had suffered a "nervous breakdown" about eighteen months before he vanished. The record also disclosed, "he was afflicted with an ailment described as loop-motor ataxia, a lack of coordination between the brain and parts of the body producing a lack of balance, among other things." Today this condition would be called cerebellar ataxia, a progressive illness that causes difficulty in coordinating the movement of hands, arms, and legs, as well as peculiarities of gait, balance issues, slurred speech, slow eye movements, and challenges with writing and eating.

Despite all of the seemingly sinister things that could have happened to the wealthy real-estate man from Lowell, the facts finally began to point to another possibility: Roger Hildreth may have simply lost his balance and taken a bad tumble.

The rest of the season passed, as did another winter and spring.

The following May brought a new crop of visitors, including nine-year-old Sulo Salmela and his twenty-two-year-old brother, Eric, who came to the park from their home in Hudson, Massachusetts. Sulo and Eric went out to explore the area around Basin Pond to attempt to find and photograph a moose, one of the most sought-after animals in the park.

Sulo suddenly saw something unusual on the ground and stopped to investigate, most likely expecting it to be the remains of a deer or even the coveted moose. Instead, he stumbled on the discovery of the year: a human skeleton.

The Salmela brothers ran for a ranger, who conducted a preliminary search of the immediate area and found a wallet with papers in it. The identification in the wallet confirmed what the ranger already guessed: The skeleton was all that remained of Roger Hildreth.

Authorities removed the body by helicopter, and state pathologist Dr. George O. Chase performed an autopsy. He said that the remains "indicate no evidence of foul play," further confirming that Hildreth's illness led him to a fall—one that, despite all the peculiar details, ended his life innocently on a May morning in 1964.

CHAPTER 5

Storm Over Fort Mountain: The Crash of a C-54

In 1940, with America's entry into World War II simply a matter of time and provocation, the Stephenville Air Force Base (AFB) in Newfoundland became a critical fuel stop for US Army Air Force planes crossing the Atlantic Ocean on their way to and from England. Positioned on a small plateau with the Long Range Mountains on one side and the Lewis Hills on the other, the AFB buzzed with activity around the clock at the height of the war. The US Army chose the tiny hamlet of Stephenville as a strategic defense position against the possibility of the Nazis establishing a beachhead on the western side of the northern Atlantic Ocean, from which the Luftwaffe—the Nazi air force—could attack the United States and the British Overseas Territories.

What began as a small base quickly grew into one of the largest and busiest US military airfields outside the United States, in part because it could accommodate the biggest military cargo planes and other major aircraft. Among these was the C-54A Skymaster, a second-generation reimagining of the Douglas DC-4 commercial passenger plane, with four added auxiliary fuel tanks—a military requirement—as well as a reinforced floor and a cargo door that operated with a winch and hoist. The plane could carry up to twenty-six passengers, making it particularly useful as a long-range transport rather than a fighter. The dependable C-54 series aircraft, manufactured in Santa Monica, California, and Cook County, Illinois, transported some of the war's top officials including President Franklin Roosevelt, General Douglas MacArthur, British Prime Minister Winston Churchill, and the armed forces of more than a dozen Allied countries.

So there was no reason to believe that the C-54A that took off from Stephenville early in the morning on June 20, 1944, would not arrive safely at its destination in Washington, DC, more or less on schedule. No reason, that is, except for the astonishing record of aircraft crashes and fatalities that the state of Maine—directly in the path of virtually every westbound or southbound flight—racked up from 1940 to 1945.

A scan of the database compiled by Peter Noddin, the master plane-wreck chaser who chronicles every known crash in his database at Aviation Archaeology in Maine (mewreckchasers .com), reveals that more than 120 people died in upwards of 420 plane crashes in Maine in these years. Hundreds of others were injured, including a number of unfortunates who happened to be at or near a crash site just as the plane went down.

Why so many? The urgency of the war effort had a lot to do with the staggering numbers of lost airmen, noted writer Rob Sneddon while examining this phenomenon for *Down East Magazine*. The need to match the enemy man for man, gun for gun, and aircraft for aircraft drove factory production and pilot training at a blistering pace. "The army didn't have the luxury of elite flight-training programs, protracted testing protocols, or patience for ideal flying conditions," Sneddon wrote. "Hundreds of thousands of airmen, many with no greater qualification than a high school diploma, were rushed through training. As soon as they reached a minimum level of competence, off they went, aboard relatively primitive, mass-produced planes that were delivered as quickly as they were riveted together."

As one of the original patriots, Benjamin Franklin, once said, "Haste makes waste." The result of this rush to put planes and pilots in the air was a fairly high level of tolerance for loss of life. Maine has more than its fair share of wrecked aircraft strewn over its mountains and driven headlong into its backcountry, rusted and charred remains that remind us of the cost of winning.

Only one of these unfortunate aircraft met its end in Baxter State Park: C-54A cargo and passenger plane #277, a mail ship with Air Transport Command's Contract Carrier #16, known outside of the war as Transcontinental & Western Air, or TWA.

A civilian captain of some renown piloted the aircraft: Roger E. "Rolley" Inman of Oskaloosa, Iowa. Not a green pilot by any stretch, forty-two-year-old Inman had enjoyed fame as a barnstormer in the 1930s, when he and his brothers, Donald and Arthur, formed the Inman Brothers Flying Circus. They performed parachute jumps and wild acrobatics in the air—and Roger's wife Margie presented one of the top acts, wing-walking on a Fokker biplane in fancy colored silks. Roger also served as an instructor with Spartan School of Aeronautics, and he and Margie achieved a different kind of infamy for owning a pet female lion named Kitty, which delighted onlookers by accompanying the couple in their travels and riding in the rumble seat of Rolley's automobile.

This thrilling pre-war life translated into some serious flying when Inman became a pilot in the war effort. He logged some 247 hours in C-54s and C-54As in the ninety days prior to June 20, 1944. In the space of six months, he had flown 210 hours at night, twenty of them in the last thirty days. If the official record is any indication, Inman had a good idea of what to expect while flying through Maine in the middle of the night. He had flown this route many times before, so he and his crew most likely expected another routine cargo mission.

Five civilian crewmen rode with him: First Officer Disbrow N. Gill, twenty-nine, of Ontario, Canada; Navigator David E. Reynolds, twenty-eight, from San Pedro, California; Nordi Byrd, a thirty-year-old engineer from Arkadelphia, Arkansas; Radio Operator Eugene B. Summers, twenty-one, of Hugoton, Kansas; and Samuel B. Berman, twenty-eight, the purser, from Washington, DC.

The only military man on board was Sargent Elbert R. Barnes, who was a passenger on the flight. The twenty-three-year-old radio operator had been stationed at Stephenville, and he took advantage of the cargo plane departing just as his leave began. He hitched a ride to Washington, DC, with the goal of making it home to his family in Escatawpa, Mississippi, later that day.

The plane departed Stephenville at 1:20 a.m. Its flight plan, filed at Stephenville before takeoff, "indicated a cruising altitude of 4000 IFR [in flight rules] and a lapse time of 6 hours and 55 minutes," the US War Department's accident report noted. "Weather reports indicated that after departure from Stephenville, flight would operate through CAVU [ceiling and visibility unrestricted] conditions until in vicinity of the Prince Edward Island, where it would begin to encounter an overcast condition with rain showers."

Flight 277 passed Moncton Radio Range Station and transmitted a report to Presque Isle Flight Control, giving its expected time of arrival over Bangor, Maine, as 4 a.m., with its final arrival in Washington, DC, four hours later. Presque Isle responded by transmitting an Army clearance to land in Washington, with instructions to contact Blissville, New Brunswick, or Bangor for airway clearance when the plane approached either station's airspace. Radio operator Summers acknowledged receipt of these instructions, and the plane continued on its route.

At 3:54 a.m., aircraft #277 checked in by radio with AA Radio WX1A in Washington. It should have contacted Blissville or Bangor radio stations moments later, but the aircraft made no contact. Hours passed with no signal.

At 10 a.m., Lieutenant Colonel C. W. Jeeter of North Atlantic Wing Operations (NAW) called headquarters and alerted them that C-54A aircraft #277 never radioed Blissville or Bangor. The news and the need for action worked its way through the layered command structure: first with a telephone call to the intelligence and security officers at Dow Field in Bangor and Presque Isle Army Air Field, who contacted local and state law enforcement, the local warning center, and anyone else in the area who might have word about the missing plane. Authorities called the Flight Control Center at Commonwealth Airport in Boston, which could offer no additional information except that Mitchell Field in New York also had attempted to contact aircraft #277 at 5 a.m. without success.

By evening on June 21, no new information had surfaced. Late that night, however, a Lieutenant Cooper at the Office of Naval Intelligence in Boston contacted the Army Air Force. He had received a report from Assistant District Coast Guard Officer Daniels, "which led the Navy to believe the 277 had been sighted or reported in the Bay of Maine." A series of phone calls clarifying the details finally led officers to decide that the sighting was false, but in the interim, the Sub Commander of the Eastern Sea Frontier took the initiative and led an "extensive search of the waters off the New England States in an effort to locate the lost aircraft. Blimps, surface patrol craft, and aircraft were employed for this mission." Even the area fishermen were engaged in maintaining a careful watch for any sign of the missing aircraft and its crew. The following day, on June 22, the Navy reported that the search had been fruitless, as the Army Air Force had predicted, and it came to an official close on June 23 at 12:20 p.m.

The inland search, however, remained stalled. The North Atlantic Wing attempted to mobilize its ground and air search operations on June 21, but low cloud cover made searching by air impossible. Later in the day, the clouds dissipated somewhat and search planes began to scour the areas around Blissville, Bangor, and Bar Harbor, but renewed cloud cover forced them back. It became clear that the overcast conditions that socked in all of the northeastern United States, Canada, and Newfoundland had most likely led the plane to make, at best, an unscheduled landing. Given the mountainous terrain it had been crossing during its last radio contact, the likelihood that the plane had found a suitable landing site was beyond remote.

But were the search planes looking in the right place? A storm could have blown the plane many miles from its original course. Officials began to narrow the parameters of the air search by using a report submitted by another pilot in the sky at just about the same time as aircraft #277.

Captain R. E. Jones, flying Contract Carrier #16, took off from Stephenville at 2:27 a.m., an hour and seven minutes after Inman departed. Jones reported that he traveled through CAVU conditions until he reached Prince Edward Island, where the sky became overcast. "In the vicinity of Moncton, Captain Jones' flight was operating through solid overcast conditions with moderate to heavy rain," the Investigating Committee paraphrased Jones' experience in its own report. Jones continued on to Blissville, and discovered that the rain and thunderstorm static "made radio reception difficult to impossible, except when in close vicinity of a radio range station."

Jones was luckier than Inman: He hit a break in the weather, making it possible for him to radio Blissville and determine that "he had been blown approximately forty miles to the North of his course while flying between Moncton and Blissville." With this information, he corrected his compass heading, and made an additional adjustment to compensate for "approximately 40 degrees of drift due to high winds along the Northeast side of the warm front that he was approaching."

He may have thought himself out of danger at this point, but halfway between Blissville and Bangor, Jones hit the center of the warm front and the worst of the storm. Rain, lightning, static, and even hail bombarded the aircraft until he found his way to the other side of the front, with only intermittent radio signals to guide him.

US Army Air Force navigators applied the drift Captain Jones had encountered to Captain Inman's flight plan, and established a ground track leading from Moncton Radio Range Station to the Katahdin region. They reported these findings to Major G. H. Shafer, chief of operations at Presque Isle Army Air Field, and he and Assistant Chief Major George E. Barnes refined their search objective to the mountains of Baxter State Park and its vicinity.

Even with this useful information, however, two more days went by before search planes could pass over Mount Katahdin safely, opening the mountains of the north woods to more thorough observation.

Major Barnes, piloting aircraft #538—a C-47 cargo plane— crested Fort Mountain at about 4 p.m. on June 23, and spotted the still-smoldering wreckage of Flight 277 near the mountain's peak. Barnes and his crew quickly established the location using Millinocket and Presque Isle as reference points, and flew in closer to search for any signs of life at the crash site.

"Careful inspection of the scene of the accident from a low altitude revealed no signs of life and appearance of the remains of the aircraft indicated almost complete destruction by crash and fire," the army's record reported. "The tail section and a short section of the fuselage aft of the cabin section was the only part of the aircraft remaining sufficiently intact to identify the wreckage as that of a C-54 aircraft."

Barnes continued to fly low to determine if there were roads or trails that would permit access to the crash site by recovery crews, and transmitted his report to Presque Isle's operations center. The army immediately dispatched a rescue and reclamation party to make their way to the accident site.

Even for the ruggedly equipped and trained ground party, however, conditions turned out to be "almost impossible," the report said. The eight-man rescue crew had to cut and blaze a new trail for nearly eight miles to reach the crash site, an effort that took another four days to complete. Finally, shortly before noon on June 27, Captain Goodale (no first name appears in the report) became the first to reach the scene of the accident.

Goodale's team now had the grisly task of inspecting the scene, making a positive identification of the aircraft, and finding the bodies of the seven people aboard among the incinerated wreckage. They began their work as a Catalina Patrol bomber dropped supplies to them in their position, about 100 feet from the 3,861-foot summit of Fort Mountain.

"Inspection of the bodies indicated that the crash caused immediate death to all on board," the report noted.

This answered the question of whether anyone could have survived the crash, but it told the initial inspectors little about what actually caused the plane to go down on Fort Mountain. The next day, an investigating committee arrived at the scene and began their forensic work. Their findings, described in fascinating—albeit disturbing—detail in their report, revealed what went wrong on the morning of June 20.

About seventy miles northwest of the Blissville-Bangor Airway, the weather changed dramatically as the C-54A encountered a "moderate to severe" thunderstorm on the edge of a warm front. Static from the lightning made it impossible for the plane to receive radio range signals or bearings, so Reynolds, the navigator, could not provide accurate information to Inman and Gill about their position in relationship to their environment. "Very strong southeast thunder storm winds were causing an excessive wind angle between its flight plan course and its actual track," the investigator's report said.

Fort Mountain loomed to the plane's starboard side, but with the wind and storm buffeting the aircraft, the radio providing no signals, and no visual cues to warn them in the storm-shrouded backcountry darkness, the crew found themselves literally flying blind. The collision, when it came, proved to be catastrophic.

Marks on the mountain indicate that the right wing was the first part of the aircraft to come in contact with the surface. The direction of the marks indicate the aircraft was flying a course of approximately 230 degrees at the instant of contact. Marks and parts of the aircraft found beyond the first point of contact show that when the right wing struck the ground the aircraft was swung approximately 15 degrees to the right. . . . [T]he aircraft crashed against large granite boulders that form a ridge extending down the Southeast corner of the mountain. When the aircraft came in contact with this rocky ridge the right wing was completely disintegrated from impact with the rocks and the forward, lower portion of the fuselage was torn away. It appears that the left wing was crumpled and that from this point on the fuselage continued with part of the crumpled left wing and plowed through large boulders and scrub trees along the side of the Mountain, a distance of approximately 1000 ft.

The plane continued to destroy itself as its momentum carried it across the mountain's surface. The nose section tore away, coming to rest about six feet before the door of the main cabin. The tail section rose upward and jammed into "a half inverted position." The fuselage burst into flames, consuming the cargo and cremating several members of the crew. Bits of the cockpit and radio controls spattered out of the aircraft on impact, cascading over the ground. "These items gave some evidence that the aircraft was being operated manually with the automatic pilot off," said the report. "The gear and flap controls were in the up position, the ADF receiver was on in the compass position and the setting on the tuning dial was approximately on the frequency of the Bangor radio range station."

While early prototypes of flight data recorders were in very limited use during World War II, such devices would not become standard until the 1960s. The C-54A had only a paper navigation log, radio log, and other flight papers on board, all of which were destroyed in the flames. None of this paperwork would have provided much in the way of clues to what exactly took place in the cockpit of aircraft #277 that morning, however. The investigative committee finally submitted this conclusion:

> *It is logical to assume that Capt. R.R. Inman in #277 encountered weather conditions as severe and possibly more severe than the conditions encountered by Capt. Jones. It is probable that any radio range or bearing signals that Capt. Inman was able to receive after passing Moncton were insufficient to give him necessary warning that extreme wind conditions prevailed along the warm front and that his tract was deviating at a wide angle from his flight plan course. . . . This condition of weather and wind accounts for the aircraft being drifted to such an extent that it arrived at the point where the accident occurred without the pilot having any knowledge that such a circumstance was developing.*

The committee completed its report with this recommendation: "If at any time the pilot is uncertain of position, such as he is unable to have proper radio reception in order to properly orientate [sic] himself, it is recommended that pilot immediately assume a cruising altitude which will clear any obstruction by 1000 feet, that is within fifty miles of either side of center of airway or ground track he intends to make good."

It took medical officers more than a week to remove the remains of the flight crew and their passenger from the wreckage, and to make formal determinations of the causes of death. On July 12, the assistant flight surgeon, Captain Joseph M. Covelli, completed his official report on each man, a gruesome catalog listing of decapitations, multiple fractures, and "total cremation" of four of the men.

Three-quarters of a century later, portions of aircraft #277 still remain in their last resting place on Fort Mountain—not because they represent a tribute to the men who died there, but because the terrain makes it virtually impossible for the park to remove them. People who want to visit the wreckage face a six-mile wilderness hike each way with no established trail, as the park has chosen not to create or maintain a trail to the site. The all-day trek summits North Brother Mountain first, then continues through dense woods with no trail markers to the summit of Fort. Finding the wreck from there is entirely a hit-and-miss enterprise.

"We would prefer if visitors set their sights on a remote pond or high mountain," said former park superintendent Jensen Bissell to writer Nick Sambides of the *Bangor Daily News* in 2009. "People who are not experienced can get in a lot of trouble. . . . You have to bushwhack to get to the last known trail point and it can take a lot of time. It is a very strenuous hike. There are a lot of gnarly mountaintops and scrubby undergrowth. It is just difficult going and it is very high, about 4,000 feet, so whatever weather you have at the beginning, you will have a lot of when you get there."

No one can say exactly how many people attempt this hike in a given year, though Bissell suggested that perhaps a dozen people a year actually visit the site. There's no denying the allure, the opportunity to step back in time and see the remains of a World War II cargo ship being slowly consumed by overgrowth and the elements. The pieces, strewn liberally over the mountainside, can be difficult to detect and may not provide as satisfying an experience as explorers may expect, Bissell noted.

"It is a pretty somber place," he told *Bangor Daily News*. "You can't get that out of your mind."

If this excursion sounds too challenging for your taste, Peter Noddin has done us the courtesy of providing photos on the

Maine Wreck Chasers website. You can see them here: mewreck chasers.com/C54A.html.

The Disappearing Piper

Even with the staggering numbers of plane crashes that took place in Maine throughout the twentieth century, only one other plane went down within the boundaries of Baxter State Park.

George Legassey and his brother, Eugene "Chink" Legassey, were both professional pilots and the proprietors of Millinocket Flying Service. On what began as a sunny Saturday on July 7, 1956, George and a passenger, Alfred "Al" McCafferty, set out in a red-and-cream Piper Cruiser equipped with pontoons over Millinocket Lake for a weekend fishing trip.

George and Al worked together on the B shift at Great Northern Paper, so they had time off from Saturday morning until late Monday afternoon. They intended to fish in the Coffeelos Pond area, some thirty-seven nautical miles north of Millinocket. George, who was thirty-four, flew over this land regularly as a guide and an officer in the Maine Civil Air Patrol (CAP). Thirty-year-old McCafferty also held a leadership position in the CAP, and his brother was an airline transatlantic transport pilot. George filed a flight plan with the Federal Aviation Administration (FAA) that specified a return date of Monday morning, July 9.

Two days passed, during which no one would expect to hear from two men on a fishing trip. Eugene Legassey took his own plane up on Sunday on other business and spotted George's Piper Cruiser at Coffeelos Pond. When he passed the area again on Monday, George's plane was gone, and Chink presumed that his brother was on his way home. He had no reason to believe that anything was amiss.

When George and Alfred did not report for their 4 p.m. shift at Great Northern Paper Company on Monday, however, the company got in touch with their families to check on their whereabouts. It didn't take long for the families to realize that something had gone wrong on the flight home.

An air search for the missing men began on July 11. Pilots from the local Maine CAP, the Shin Pond Squadron of the CAP, and Presque Isle and Loring Air Force bases, as well as the Air Force Rescue Service in Westover, Massachusetts, all mobilized to canvass the treetops throughout Township 6, Range 11—the area around Coffeelos—with no success. On the third day of the search, Ivan McCafferty, Alfred's brother and a trans-oceanic pilot stationed at what was then Idlewild (now John F. Kennedy) Airport in New York, arrived in Millinocket to assist. "For some time the search was concentrated around Frost Lake, Rainbow Lake, Chesuncook Pond and an area above Ripogenus Dam," the *Bangor Daily News* reported. On July 13, the operation turned to the west as a source reported to the local CAP that "a plane believed to be Legassey's had been sighted flying in the rain Monday," according to a report in the *Lewiston Evening Journal*. The searchers focused their efforts on the lower halves of Chensuncook and Lobster Lakes, west of Mount Katahdin. According to the *Evening Journal*'s report, Colonel Arthur L. Patstone, the CAP communications officer, told the media that fifteen search aircraft made twenty-three sorties on July 12.

Leaders of the search effort formulated a working theory of what had happened to the plane. They believed that the missing pilot—whom, they agreed, could have been either George or Al—may have run into "a solid wall of fog" on his way back from Coffeelos on Monday, and that he changed course and turned north to try to go around it. This may have resulted in a crash somewhat north of their original intended route. While there was no way to know if this theory was accurate, it at least gave the searchers some parameters within which to look for the downed plane.

As the week wore on, the searchers followed up on every tip they received from local residents. One reported seeing a low-flying plane over the Moosehead region around the time that

Legassey's plane was believed to have disappeared. Another said she heard a plane turning north in the fog over Frost Pond on July 9, seeming to bear out the theory that the pilot had changed course because of weather. The entire search effort—by this time including twenty-seven planes from several Maine Civil Air Patrol units and the Air Force Rescue Service—shifted to cover that section. Even with this well-organized search and so many planes and helicopters in the air, however, no one saw so much as a glint of metal or a flash of red in the treetops below.

Then the rain came. Search planes were grounded for more than a day, and questions began to arise about the cost of the fuel and other expenses the CAP and Air Force were racking up as the effort wore on. Townspeople in Millinocket got together and raised $300 to defray the gasoline cost, and another $1,881.31 for food, lodging, and other expenses. Even with this encouragement and assistance from the public, however, leaders of the search eventually had to call it quits. On July 15, the Civil Air Patrol called off further sorties, and the Westover Base ended its efforts as well. Together they had combed three thousand square miles of forested area, ponds, and lakes, and they had not turned up a single clue.

Both Legassey and McCafferty were married, and Legassey had one son, while another was born shortly after he disappeared. McCafferty had two sons of his own. Their wives remarried and raised their children, and more than a decade went by with no opportunity for closure. It seemed that there would never be more information about the two pilots and their ill-fated fishing trip.

Then on a clear May 14 in 1968—nearly twelve years after the Piper disappeared—Maine Fish and Game Warden Andrew Stinson flew over Sourdnahunk Field and glimpsed something he had never seen there before. He radioed Richard Rideout, Millinocket chief of police, that he believed he had seen the remains of a crashed plane. Rideout contacted Eugene Legassey, and Legassey flew over the field accompanied by Dr. Herbert C.

Gilman of Millinocket later the same day. Legassey "said he was 99 percent sure that the wreckage was that of the plane that his brother and Alfred McCafferty, 30, were in," the *Bangor Daily News* reported.

On Wednesday, Legassey and members of the Millinocket Search and Rescue unit drove to Sourdnahunk Field and walked into the wilderness for three miles to the crash site, south of Sourdnahunk Stream and about a mile north of Brothers Mountain. Here Legassey confirmed that the wreckage was the lost Piper Cruiser.

"They apparently got disoriented trying to find the river in poor weather and struck a pine tree on the ridge," said Peter Noddin of the Maine Wreck Chasers website, corresponding with me by e-mail.

He also shared another story that had gone almost unnoticed by the media: "An Air Force captain named Campbell Potter from the 42nd FMS [Field Maintenance Squadron] at Loring Air Force Base was assigned to fly search missions for [Legassey and McCafferty] with a C-54 out of Millinocket until the search was called off," he said. "Being heavily involved with CAP himself, he took his annual leave and flew his Howard aircraft (in CAP colors) to Millinocket and continued the search on his own nickel. He died attempting an emergency landing at Millinocket a few days before Christmas that winter." Lieutenant Donald N. Stacey, also in the plane, was injured in that crash on December 21, 1956.

Such is the sense of fellowship between members of search-and-rescue organizations, who will go the extra mile for one of their own even when it can mean risking their own lives.

CHAPTER 6

The Murderous Phantom
of the Allagash

Dear Readers: Of all the stories I encountered while researching this book, none has taken on the patina of legend like the murder of Wesley Porter. I have done my best to reconstruct this tale as factually and thoroughly as I can, using written accounts found in the media, on the web, and in books written by Maine fish and game wardens over the course of more than seventy years. Many of these accounts were based on descriptions and notes from actual participants in the manhunt. If you know of facts that I've missed here, let's keep the process going: Contact me at author@minetor.com and share what you know, and I will continue to compile information for this book's next edition.

IN THE STILL OF A MAINE NORTH COUNTRY NIGHT, AT A STATE forest camp near Webster Lake in Northern Piscataquis county, three men from Massachusetts and their highly experienced guide relaxed comfortably in the gathering twilight after supper. Robert Hames and William Buchanan of Athol and Robert Jarvis of Greenfield had engaged the services of one of the best known and most highly recommended of the Maine Guides, Wesley Porter, for the pleasure of fishing in the early days of June 1943. Porter, a potato farmer from Patten, Maine, had earned a solid reputation as one of the most experienced and skilled guides visitors to the densely forested north country could want.

They had met in Sherman on May 31, traveled to Grand Lake Dam by taxi, and spent the night there, taking a boat the next morning to Second Lake. Here they placed a cache of supplies at a lumber office and packed just what they needed for the next day or two into their camp. They moved up Webster Stream to the camp at Webster Lake.

Webster Lake serves as the headwaters of the East Branch of the Penobscot River, covering about 530 square acres in the northernmost part of Baxter State Park. Today Wadleigh Mountain Road takes visitors to a high-clearance dirt road that leads directly to the campsite at Webster Outlet, but in Wesley Porter's day, a trail worn clear of vegetation by the boots of fishermen and hunters provided the only route from Second Lake to Webster Lake.

On June 2, they had prepared their camp for a stay of several days and got ready for a week of fishing. Thursday morning found them at Coffeelos Lake, where the Massachusetts visitors fished while Porter hiked back out to Second Lake to pick up their cache of additional supplies. He returned to the camp at about 5:30 p.m., and as they made their supper and shared stories of the day's fishing, Porter asked if they had gone as far as Telos Dam at the western end of Webster Lake. The men noted that they had not, and wondered why he asked. Porter told them that someone had been seen around that area. He may not have shared, however, that there had been a series of break-ins at camps in the area since spring, and that food and supplies had been stolen during these incidents. In several cases, shotgun blasts had shattered cabin windows.

The evening progressed peacefully enough after dinner. Jarvis went looking for bait, crouching on a ledge above the water to watch for minnows. Hames and Buchanan watched idly until a scratching sound behind the camp caught their attention.

Both men picked up their .22 caliber revolvers and circled the camp in opposite directions, watching for movement among the trees and understory and expecting a porcupine, an animal that either of them would have enjoyed bringing home as a trophy of their trip. As they moved around the camp, they left Porter standing alone.

No one expected to hear gunshots—first one, a pause, and then one more. Jarvis ducked under the ledge and crouched there, waiting for more gunfire. Buchanan and Hames moved as swiftly and quietly as they could back to the front of the camp.

They were unprepared for what they found there. Wesley Porter lay on the ground, rolling from side to side, bleeding profusely from wounds in his head.

Their first assumption was that Porter had somehow shot himself accidentally. "My God, Wes, what have you done?" Buchanan said aloud.

Then to their amazement, a third shot rang out from outside the camp. Now Buchanan and Hames instantly revised their guess, believing that the shots were coming from a set gun—a gun set to fire when prey touches a wire attached to the trigger. Such a method was used by some hunters to take down game, or in wartime to ward off an enemy intruder.

Now Jarvis returned to camp as quickly as he could, and he and Hames provided first aid to Porter while Buchanan called for help on a telephone line near the camp, placed there for use by the state and Great Northern Paper Company. He contacted the caretaker at Telos Dam, who relayed him to Greenville, about one hundred miles to the southwest, where Dr. J. F. Pritham was dispatched by a state forestry plane piloted by Earl Miller to the camp. He arrived quickly as twilight turned to darkness, but there was nothing he could do for Porter. The *Bangor Daily News* reported what Dr. Pritham shared: At 12:20 a.m., Porter breathed his last.

Porter, who was forty-six years old, left behind a wife and seven children, two of whom were soldiers serving overseas at the height of World War II.

Pritham also served as the area medical examiner, so it fell to him to perform the autopsy and determine the exact cause of death. On June 4, the day after the shooting, a plane piloted by Ray O'Donnell flew Porter's body to Harvey's funeral home in Greenville. At the end of a long day and a detailed examination of the body, Dr. Pritham announced to the media that the bullet that killed Wesley Porter "was fired at him deliberately."

Sheriff Thomas L. Foulkes of Porter provided the details of the fatal wound. He said that the bullet "entered his head behind his left ear and lodged in his brain," the Associated Press reported. "A second bullet struck Porter's upper lip, knocking out two front teeth, and the third grazed the back of his neck." The *Bangor Daily News* added details from Dr. Pritham: The bullet that entered his head had exploded into fragments inside his brain, a discovery that had considerably lengthened the time of the autopsy.

"Dr. Pritham said the bullets were of a small, high explosive type with silver tip and clover-leaf jackets," the *Bangor Daily News* added.

Early on the morning of June 4, the Piscataquis County Sheriff's Office and Maine State Police began their investigation. Lieutenant Miller of the Civil Air Patrol flew Deputy Sheriff David Knowlton and State Trooper James Mealy to the campsite. There, a search turned up an exploded twenty-gauge shotgun shell and "a number of shots embedded in trees," noted an account of the search written in 2009 by Maine State Trooper Mark Nickerson on a Wesley Porter tribute website. (Nickerson worked from notebooks provided by commanding officer Lieutenant Merle E. Cole and case notes from his own father, Captain Millard E. "Nick" Nickerson, who became the director of the Bureau of Criminal Investigations of the Maine State Police.) Knowlton walked six miles Friday afternoon to the Eastern Manufacturing Company lumber camp, but he did not locate the killer. By evening, an electrical storm pinned down Knowlton and Mealy at Webster Lake.

Returning to Dover-Foxcroft on Saturday morning, Knowlton, Cole, Mealy, and Sargent Arthur Freeman from Augusta headquarters detained the three fishermen who were with Porter for lengthy questioning, keeping them at the courthouse from 8 p.m. on Saturday until Sunday at 7 a.m. They were soon cleared of any wrongdoing, however, as a twenty-gauge shotgun had been determined to be the murder weapon, and none of them carried such a gun. Law-enforcement officials told the media that the three fishermen told the same story that had been recorded in their signed statements at Webster Lake late Thursday night. "Reports of investigations by the Massachusetts State Police showed them to be of good character," wrote Nickerson.

With no question that a murderer was at large somewhere in the north woods, Deputy Chief Laurence C. Upton of the Maine State Police ordered a roadblock at the Shin Pond Outlet, the only way a man could take on foot or by boat to leave the vicinity. Lieutenant Cole arrived at the scene in a plane supplied by the Inland Fish and Game Department. He directed two troopers, Charles Marks and Lloyd Hoxie, to take boats and search the lakeshore for the murder weapon.

The list of possible suspects began to grow. Porter had a nephew who had a conviction on his record for poaching in New Hampshire. A German man in the area who was already under investigation for "subversive activities" also attracted suspicion, as the nation was firmly in the grip of World War II fervor. As the investigation brought more physical evidence to light in the form of hair particles, bits of clothing, and descriptions of unusual characters seen by residents of camps around Webster Lake and others nearby, however, the field narrowed significantly. Trooper Mealy discovered a shotgun cartridge and twenty-eight buckshot that had been fired recently near the camp where Porter had been shot, in a clump of Norway pines.

While Porter's family held his funeral on June 9 in Patten and laid him to rest in the town cemetery, the investigation continued to the north. The *Lewiston Daily Sun* reported that Piscataquis County attorney Jerome Clark requested of the county commissioners that the troopers have a plane to transport officers to and from the crime scene, to speed up their efforts to find the killer. Without a plane, the investigation would be slow as troopers and other officers would have to proceed on foot.

Over time, the search for clues resulted in enough fragments of evidence for investigators to put together a description of the man for whom they were searching. They believed the man was hunting illegally in the area, and that he was responsible for a series of break-ins that had begun during the winter of 1942 and 1943. "The path of the thief seemed to be heading north," wrote Nickerson. "At a break-in at a camp on Chamberlain Lake, a 20-gauge shell was found, and ballistics showed it to be identical with that found at the scene of the murder. Clothing was seized and the State Bureau of Identification drew a description of the wanted man. This description was forwarded to all area law enforcement officers, guides and hunters."

As June wore on and the shooter still had not been found, the trail seemed to grow cold. Perhaps the man in the woods realized that he had become the target of law enforcement and found a way to lie low, or he became more skillful at covering his own tracks. For whatever reason, the investigation began to flag. Not until the middle of July did the search for the killer get a sudden surge of renewed vigor.

"By Attorney General Frank I. Cowan's orders," the Associated Press reported on July 15, "the body of Wesley F. Porter . . . was exhumed from Patten's town cemetery today and taken to Augusta for an autopsy."

This second autopsy would be performed by Dr. Arch H. Morrell, Maine's state pathologist. Cowan told the media he wanted this additional examination "so we may be prepared to answer any questions anytime."

At the end of the day on July 15, after beginning the process of examining the exhumed body, Dr. Morrell told media that he would not complete the autopsy until the following week. "It looks like a long job," he said. When he finally finished the gruesome task, he confirmed what the first autopsy had revealed: The death was indeed a deliberate act by someone who had taken aim at Porter's head.

With no new information gained from the second autopsy, it's not clear from news reports exactly what transpired next to recharge the hunt, but Maine Game Warden Eric Wight suggests a reason in his book, *Life and Death in the North Woods: The Story of the Maine Game Warden Service*. He spoke with former warden supervisor Helon Taylor—the one for whom the trail to Mount Katahdin is named—who was in service when the manhunt took place.

Taylor said that about a month into the search for Porter's killer, he himself was called into the state police headquarters in Augusta to share a theory he had. "I told him that during World War I, many Canadians had hidden out in the woods around Eustis and Chain of Ponds to avoid conscription into the Canadian army," he said. "My theory was that this was a similar case."

Maine Commissioner of Inland Fisheries and Game George Stobie told Taylor to "take some wardens and bring him out," and Taylor assembled a team including Wardens Bert Duty, Charlie Harriman, and several others. They flew out to Nugent's Camps on Chamberlain Lake, where they found that the fugitive, whoever he was, had preceded their arrival. "It, too, had been broken into and food stolen, along with a 20-gauge shotgun," Taylor told Wight. "Other camps in the area on Snake Pond, Carpenter Pond, and Hudson Pond had all been broken into, and all shared the shotgun blast through the window." They found the same thing at Clear Lake Camp, where warden Charlie Harriman's coat had been stolen as well.

On the night of July 31, while Duty and another warden camped in the Warden Camp on Soper Mountain, they took special precautions not to attract the attention of the killer—especially after a Great Northern Paper Company forester told them that he had seen the man in the area. The wardens slept inside the cabin without using any lights, but when Duty lit a match to have a smoke, someone in the woods fired a single shot through the window. Duty hit the floor and was lucky enough to have the bullet miss him and hit the telephone on the cabin wall, essentially destroying it.

He quickly fired his gun into the woods in the direction of the shot. He did not hit his assailant, who slipped away into the darkness, but Duty found the shell from the shot that had come so close to him. It was identical to the two already in hand as evidence.

The new altercation brought the entire weight of every form of law enforcement down onto the area around Soper Mountain. Twenty-four-hour surveillance made it impossible for the perpetrator to move freely in the woods. Duty and Taylor soon found the killer's camp, but he had abandoned it "and was apparently living in the swampland," Nickerson wrote.

The break in the case brought new resources to the searchers. The Connecticut State Police sent two bloodhounds and their handlers on the afternoon of August 7, and the dogs picked up the killer's scent that evening. They tracked him until dark and determined that he made regular use of the trail between Fourth and Third Masquascook Lakes. Clinton Porter, Wesley's sixteen-year-old son, and family friend Albert C. "Chub" Foster, himself a Maine Guide and the owner of the Matagamon Camp near Webster Lake, stationed themselves in the brush just off the trail at daybreak on August 8 to watch for the man's first movements of the day. They had orders from the sheriff to "shoot on sight, but not to kill the suspect," according to the *Boston Globe*.

It didn't take long for the suspect to emerge. Clinton Porter and Foster heard a noise at about 10 a.m. and spotted a man coming down the trail from the general direction of Clear Mountain. He had long, black hair, and the lower half of his face was covered with a thick, four-inch-long black beard. He was wearing a warden's coat and carrying a pack, an axe . . . and a single-barrel, twenty-gauge shotgun.

The two men let him come within about twenty feet of them before Foster spoke up. "Just a minute, mister," he said, and stepped out from his hiding place.

The startled suspect dropped the axe and began to take aim with his shotgun. He wasn't fast enough, however, and Foster took his shot first, hitting the man in the right thigh.

"For a few moments, the man didn't see Foster, toward whom he was walking," reported Maine Chief Fish and Game Warden Earle Bradbury to the media later that day. "Suddenly he looked up and, seeing Foster, pulled up his shotgun and swung toward Foster. Foster let him have it in the leg in self-defense."

Foster and Porter administered first aid to the wound and attempted to carry the man out of the forest, but a warden in a plane overhead spotted them on the shore of Musquacook Lake and landed, picking up the wounded man and flying him to the hospital in Greenville and arriving there at about 1:40 p.m.

Soon Lieutenant Cole appeared and arrested the suspect. He discovered quickly that the man spoke French but no English, so the subsequent interrogation involved an interpreter. Cole learned that the man's name was Alphonse Morency (sources differ on the spelling of his name, some choosing Morencé or Mauricé in a nod to his French Canadian background), he was from Sainte-Sabien in the Canadian province of Quebec, and he had lived in the woods for more than a year, since June 1942. He had opted for this fugitive lifestyle to avoid being drafted into the armed forces and sent off to Europe to fight in the war.

If his objection to military service had to do with being a pacifist, Morency had clearly discarded that romantic notion once he took up residence in the woods. He survived by breaking into other people's camps and stealing food and clothing, as well as the shotgun and shells he had used when he killed Wesley Porter.

The murder, however, apparently had been a sort of accident. Morency explained that he had fired into camps at Webster Lake, Clear Lake, and Soper Mountain to make sure that there were no people in them before he entered and conducted his heists. He said he made a point of shooting high in the air to avoid hitting anyone, but on the evening of June 3, 1943, this strategy had not worked in his favor.

"I fired to the side of two men close to a camp," he is said to have told law enforcement. "I know I didn't hit them but they ran in the directions of my shots. There were talking, excited talking, so I immediately continued on. If I hit someone else I didn't know it." (This quote, however, comes from the February 1944 edition of *True Detective*, a pulp magazine full of dramatized accounts of actual criminal investigations, and may be more fiction than fact.)

Whether Morency actually knew that he had shot and killed Porter is not absolutely clear from the media reports. "He had no recollection of the time of that shooting, or of its time relationship to another shooting he confessed to at Clair [sic] Lake," the *Boston Globe* reported. Indeed, given the man's depleted physical condition, more than a year in the woods without a calendar or a watch, and the loss of blood from his fresh wound, it was difficult to know what he remembered of his actions. He did know officers with bloodhounds had begun to pursue him the night before his capture, however, and he chose the trail on which he had been apprehended because he could move quickly on it, hoping to elude the dogs and their handlers.

Six hours after he was shot, at about 4 p.m., Morency succumbed to his wound and passed away. Dr. Pritham said that the man's death was due to the loss of blood, but that his weakened condition after more than a year of living hand to mouth in the woods played a role in his death as well.

"Knowlton said he was sure Morency was the man whose trail had been followed through some of the wildest country in northern Maine by more than fifty state police, fish and game wardens, woodsmen, and guides," the *Bangor Daily News* reported on August 9, after the man died.

Indeed, with Morency no longer in the woods, the break-ins at camps ceased and there were no more shots fired through cabins in the darkness. Peace returned to the north country, and while this is no longer the longest manhunt in Maine history (it was eclipsed in 2017 by the search for a murderer in Parkman), it remains a tale told around campfires, spun into legend, and embellished by the decades.

CHAPTER 7

The 4,700-Foot February Bivouac

Members of the Appalachian Mountain Club (AMC) are a particularly hardy group. The nearly 150-year-old organization has built its reputation on promoting the freedom to explore the wilderness while practicing "safe and environmentally responsible outdoor recreation," according to the AMC's current website at outdoors.org. Active members often participate in adventures throughout the region—from Maine to Washington, DC—that are run by experienced leaders and guides who teach wilderness skills in all kinds of terrain. In particular, the AMC's headquarters at Pinkham Notch, New Hampshire, provides the information and skill-building opportunities that hikers and climbers need before they brave the extreme weather on Mount Washington, the tallest and most treacherous mountain in the northeastern United States.

So when six young AMC members from across the New England states set out to climb Mount Katahdin on an unseasonably warm January day, they knew the kind of challenges they might encounter. All but one of them had climbed rugged ice and snow gullies in winter—and two of the men had completed winter ice climbs on Katahdin as recently as the year before. They were well equipped with ropes and the necessary climbing equipment, and food for a twelve- to eighteen-hour day on the mountain in the height of the annual January thaw. Temperatures were in the forties as they readied for the climb in their cabin on the morning of January 31, 1974. It looked like a grand day for a technical climb to Pamola Peak.

Twenty-five-year-old Bob Proudman, the expedition leader, came to Katahdin from Gorham, New Hampshire, and he brought the widest breadth of experience to the party. His skill in technical climbing had made him something of a legend among AMC members; he had become the first to scale a number of mountains in winter and had plunged fearlessly into stormy conditions on at least one occasion. Now that he had reached his mid-twenties, however, he had had enough close calls to know that he was not indestructible. He put safety before stunts, especially when he took the leadership position on a climb.

Mike Cohen, who was thirty and from Brighton, Massachusetts, had taken up ice climbing in 1972 and often climbed with Bob. Twenty-three-year-old Paul DiBello of Jackson, New Hampshire, had turned to ice climbing after years of skiing for the rush of being "on the edge," as he told *New England Today* magazine decades later. Page Dinsmore, the youngest in the expedition at nineteen years old, had grown up in Shelburne, New Hampshire, where the White Mountains offered him plenty of opportunity for rock scrambling and other tests of his skill and agility. The Katahdin climb would be his first major ice climb, though his upbringing in the Appalachian Mountain region left him with no fear of winter conditions. Doug George from Concord, New Hampshire, had started skiing at age three, and now, at twenty-three, had climbed Katahdin in winter with Bob Proudman the year before.

Twenty-six-year-old Tom Keddy of Wakefield, Massachusetts, loved to ski and moved to Pinkham Notch upon his discharge from the US Navy, where he met Bob and began ice climbing with him. He was a last-minute addition to the Katahdin expedition when another climber had to cancel; this was his first visit to the snow and ice gullies on Maine's highest mountain.

Their chosen climb involved a 2,200-foot rise to Pamola Peak, scaling two gullies on the cliff of the same name. They awoke to a mild, sunny morning—the tenth in succession in the annual January thaw—and they judged the day's likely weather forecast by the red morning sky and the bank of clouds on the distant horizon. Bob recognized the signs that bad weather was approaching, but he believed that it would not arrive until evening or later. They had no radio to tell them differently.

What they did not know was that the Portland Weather Bureau had issued a forecast early that morning that may well have stopped them from venturing onto Katahdin: "HIGH WIND WARNING IN EFFECT LATE TODAY. MOSTLY SUNNY THIS MORNING. INCREASING CLOUDINESS THIS AFTERNOON WITH A CHANCE OF SNOW BY EVENING FOLLOWED BY CLEARING. HIGHS AROUND 50. MUCH COLDER WITH LOWS 5 TO 10 TONIGHT."

Even this might not have curtailed their plans, as they expected to return from their climb before nightfall. None of them had any intention of spending a night on Katahdin.

They had breakfast and dressed in full winter climbing regalia including wool pants and shirts, double boots and hats, wind pants, gaiters, and windbreakers. Each of the men had a sweater and a down vest in his pack, and Bob and Page carried expedition parkas. They planned to return before dark, so they did not carry sleeping bags, emergency shelter, or food and water beyond what they needed for an eight-hour climb.

Once they arrived at the mountain at about 9:30 a.m., the men split into two groups of three. Paul led the rope-one trio including Page and Tom, while Doug and Mike followed Bob on rope two. Each group chose a gully to climb and began the laborious process of making their way up the rock wall. Soon Bob's group was far ahead of Paul's, as the men on rope one found the going "straight forward, making good progress," according to the accident report written by American Alpine Club member George Hamilton. Bob's gully held considerably more snow than ice, making the going fairly swift and less challenging than Paul's gully—what Paul would later describe as "the best ice of my life" consisted of refrozen meltwater, a particularly challenging form that made for slow going.

Bob's trio stopped for lunch at about 2 p.m., and looked back to see how far the rope two group had come. They could not see their friends, but they knew that the climbing in the second gully was more difficult than the one they had selected. With hunger satisfied after the brief stop, Bob led his group farther up the mountain over mixed snow and ice and bare rock—but even as he knew that he'd chosen the faster route, he became concerned that their progress was not as rapid as they all had intended. Toward late afternoon, as he ascended into the clouds near the summit, he realized that Pamola Peak was still some distance away and they would not be able to make it there before dark.

It had been hours since the two groups had communicated with one another, but as night began to set in around 5 p.m., Bob called out to Paul's group and got no answer through the gloom. By this time fog had set in as well, so visual contact was not possible.

After a time, Paul shouted to Bob that he thought his group was about twenty minutes from Bob's location, and asked his group to wait for them to catch up. Paul said that he and his two companions only had one headlamp between them, so their going would be even slower than it had been all day. Worse, they had not stopped for lunch, so fatigue and hunger had begun to sap their strength. Bob's team agreed to wait, though Bob believed that twenty minutes would not be long enough for the second team to reach them.

Sure enough, nearly three hours passed before Paul, Page, and Tom came close enough to be seen. By this time Bob had taken the initiative to place two rock pins in the snow and cut a platform where they could all spend the night, choosing a ledge at about

4,700 feet—500 feet from the summit. Fog and mist shrouded the peak above them, so none of the three waiting men could see what might lie ahead between their perch and the peak. Bob began to feel uneasy as the weather grew eerily still.

The real threat, however, was not in what might be before them on their route to the mountaintop. Throughout the day temperatures had held in the mid-forties, so the men were dressed for this weather and for the exertion of climbing. They had purposely packed lightly so a heavy load would not hinder their efforts.

In short, none of them were ready for the storm.

It came in a sudden rush of wind, driving a torrent of snow into their faces and robbing their bodies of natural warmth. In what seemed like no time, the temperature dropped more than fifty degrees. The storm blasted through northern New England and made itself the stuff of legend. "It tore roofs off of mobile homes and tossed them into nearby trees, and sent tree limbs crashing into power lines, leaving thousands of homes without electricity," wrote Mel Allen in a 1980 issue of *Yankee* magazine.

The six men clung to the mountain for what shelter they could find on their perches, with three of them still climbing to the ledge where Bob waited for them. Lightning flashed and thunder boomed around them as the massive cold front slammed into the warmer air that had enveloped the mountain for more than a week. For two interminable hours, the snow fell so swiftly and in such quantity that the men had to hide their faces to escape smothering.

When the snow finally slowed, Doug and Page worked their way up to the ledge Bob had created, and Mike, Paul, and Tom soon followed. "George had just dropped a (150 foot) rope to Dinsmore [when the storm hit]," the AAC report said. "Dinsmore was leading the other rope still and was climbing directly behind George. Dinsmore, too, needed some assistance on the last thirty feet of the pitch. In short order, Mike, Paul, and Tom reached what was to prove to be the bivouac site for the night."

After such a strenuous day with no rest or food, all three men needed help to reach the five-foot ledge on which they came to rest, but Tom seemed particularly exhausted. He repeatedly lost his grip and his footing in scrambling up to the ledge. "DiBello's team was in poorer condition than the other, having found the going difficult in spots and making slower progress," the AAC report says, basing its observations on Hamilton's interviews with the men after the incident. "Dinsmore feels that all three were feeling some effects of hypothermia. Paul did not have his expedition parka and Keddy could not get his wind pants on; he had not been able to get his Dacron parka on alone. It took Proudman and one other forty-five minutes to help Keddy don his parka."

It was close to midnight when all six men were finally reunited on the narrow ledge and tied securely to the rock anchor pins Bob had driven hours earlier. Now they had a terrifying task ahead of them: staying awake despite the day's exertions, and resisting the frigid temperatures—with wind chills bottoming out to eighty degrees below zero—swirling snow, and gale force winds in the impenetrable darkness of a mountain wilderness night. Attempting to climb down looked like suicide to Bob, as a slip could send all three men on a rope to their deaths on the jagged rocks below. The ropes they had used on the way up sat in a hopeless tangle on the ledge. Making their way down in the dark simply wasn't an option.

The men huddled close to one another, using their body heat to keep everyone as warm as possible as the night wore on. They ate what food they could retrieve from their packs in the cramped space, generating additional energy to bear the freezing gusts that battered them—some as hard as one hundred miles per hour—and the penetrating cold as it dropped to minus twenty-five degrees. They sang songs to maintain morale, screamed "Endure!" into the wind in a gallant chorus, moved numb fingers and toes to keep blood flowing, and called out one another's names to make sure that no one fell asleep. So tight was their space on the ledge that they could not even get their sweaters out of their packs.

"After huddling together for some time, they tried to get on their feet to assess their conditions," Hamilton wrote. "DiBello was unable to stand." He had lost feeling in his legs and feet.

So they passed the hours until light returned, when they could finally see one another and determine what toll the long, exposed night had taken. "Each was appalled as he looked at his companions," the AAC report said. "All were suffering from frostbite. Dinsmore said that he had to leave immediately because he was freezing to death." Bob agreed with him, even though it meant that Page would be climbing down through the gully—a fifth-class climb, making it one of the toughest in the region— unaided and alone. Remarkably, the wind came to his aid in this case, racing upward in the gully and buoying him up as he worked his way down.

All five of the remaining men realized that their eyesight was compromised, the result of frostbitten eyeballs. Mike and Bob set to work attempting to free the tangled ropes used in the upward climb, to help themselves and the others make their way up to the ridge, now well within sight, where they could walk the Dudley Trail back to Chimney Pond Camp.

"Our plan was for me to climb out 150 feet of this line and to wait while Cohen pulled and cut the longest stretch of rope he could find in the tangle," Bob told the AAC writer. "He would then tie this stretch onto the end of the line going to me. I could then climb out until the rope was again taut, at which time another stretch would be pulled out, cut by Mike, and tied onto my line. The plan was to repeat the process until we had a line attached to the ridge connecting it with the bivouac site. With this hand line we hoped we'd all be able to get off the technical stuff and onto the ridge."

The slope between the bivouac and the ridge tilted at a steep sixty-degree angle, but Bob managed to make his way to the ridge.

He tied off his rope on a large boulder. "He rappelled swiftly down the cliff, exulting that they would all soon be out, when suddenly he was clutching the end of the rope, dangling over space; the knots had untied in the wind," Allen wrote in *Yankee*. "He hung onto the rope for what seemed an eternity. He couldn't see. He yelled for Mike but he knew it was futile. He wondered if he could even find the ledge; he knew it might be suicidal to climb down with blurred vision, with no rope anchoring him to the mountain. He decided to leave, hoping there was time for a rescue. 'I wish I could have told them that it was probably, here on in, every man for himself,' he says."

Bob made his way back up to the ridge and began the comparatively simple hike down, made far more difficult than usual by his weakened condition. To his relief, he soon came upon Page. The young climber had reached a large boulder along the trail and huddled behind it for shelter from the wind, but when he saw Bob, he agreed gladly to continue down the trail with him. They reached Taylor Trail junction and turned in the wrong direction, but they realized their error and bushwhacked their way back to the Chimney Pond Trail by 2:30 p.m. The additional effort nearly depleted their last stores of energy, but the prospect of reaching camp and finding help kept them moving.

They decided to continue down the trail toward Roaring Brook Camp, rather than turning toward Chimney Pond Camp. As they approached Roaring Brook, they spotted Ranger Arthur York's personal snowmobile, and Bob sent Page on to the camp to get help from the rangers there. Bob turned around and started back up the trail to Chimney Pond.

Meanwhile, Mike and Doug, still sitting on the ledge, realized when the rope to the ridge went slack that something had gone wrong with the plan. They worked for as long as they could to share what little body heat they had remaining with Paul and Tom, but their own strength had waned until they knew they had to move or succumb to the wind and cold.

Mike decided the time had come to go, and Doug agreed. They told Paul they were going for help, and slowly, painfully, and without a rope to assist them, they made their way up to the ridge toward the Dudley Trail.

"On his way to the ridge, Doug's glove blew away as he momentarily placed it under his arm," Allen wrote. "He screamed watching his hand shrivel in sixty seconds. Miraculously the glove blew past Mike, then when the wind slackened, slid back down. Using his teeth, Mike tugged the glove over Doug's now useless hand. When he reached the ridge Doug walked around in circles until he came to his senses and started down Dudley Trail."

With his last reserves of strength, Doug made it to Chimney Pond, crawling the last hundred yards to the ranger cabin. He pounded on the door and Ranger York opened it, discovering for the first time that the climbing expedition had gone horribly wrong. Ten minutes later, Mike staggered into the ranger station as well . . . and as York began to administer first aid, word came from Roaring Brook Camp that Page had managed to reach the ranger cabin there, broken in, and radioed for help.

Bob, still making his way to Chimney Pond, soon ran into Ranger York looking for him. Now Bob received the happy news that Mike and Doug had made their way down to Chimney Pond as well and were receiving first aid there. York helped him to the ranger cabin, and he and his wife gave first aid to all three men while they waited for a rescue helicopter to arrive.

Rescue personnel in the chopper went first to pick up Page at Roaring Brook. They delivered him to Millinocket Hospital and took off again, battling high winds and blowing snow to reach Chimney Pond and bring out Bob, Mike, and Doug.

As far as anyone knew at that point, Paul and Tom remained on the mountain, and the park began to plan the best course for a rescue.

Paul, determined to save himself and his friend, stayed with Tom while he slipped in and out of consciousness and managed to keep him in a sitting position, pulling him upright again and again to prevent his falling off the ledge. "The body is resourceful," Allen wrote. "By cutting off blood to Paul's feet and legs, more blood flowed to his brain and he started to think clearly. When he felt his hands also begin to freeze he became scared, and realized his hopes for rescue were remote."

If there was any chance that he could save Tom's life as well as his own, Paul was ready to take it. "It's time to go!" he yelled at Tom. "We're not going to stay here and die." Tom could barely respond, and it was clear that he could not move, much less climb his way to the ridge.

Finally, certain that he had to leave or perish, Paul spent two hours trying to slap and rub some sensation into his legs. He forced himself to a standing position, and used one of the last remaining rope fragments to attempt to pull Tom with him to the ridge. In his depleted state, however, he had no hope of carrying Tom's weight with his own. He finally made the wrenching decision to secure Tom to one of the anchors, leave him at the site, and proceed alone.

Paul left the bivouac at about 3:30 p.m. Through frostbitten eyes he could not see much beyond a wall of white, but he groped his way up to the ridge, prevented from falling by the fierce winds that kept him moving upward even when he lost his footing. He reached the ridge, facing into the wind to hold himself to a southwest bearing, knowing that this was the direction of Chimney Pond Camp. Before long, however, his lack of clear eyesight became a serious hazard, and he strayed from the trail, forced to use his limited strength to bushwhack his way through the scrub below the ridge. Suddenly he felt no ground beneath his feet. He fell through clear air into deep snow and spruce branches, twigs scratching at his eyes and robbing him of some of his remaining sight. Even his ice axe disappeared into the void below him.

Somehow he got to his feet and made his way back to the ridge. This time he managed to stay on the trail and crawled his way down the mountain until he saw a light in the distance—a lamp in the ranger cabin at Chimney Pond Camp. Heartened by this evidence that he was not the only person on the mountain, he continued to crawl until he bumped smack into the cabin and deposited himself on its doorstep at about 7 p.m.

Ranger York and his wife pulled him into the cabin and began immediate care for Paul's frostbite, exposure, and exhaustion as Paul gave in to unconsciousness at last. They made him as comfortable as they could and provided first aid until he could be airlifted out of the park.

With five of the six men retrieved from Mount Katahdin, rescue efforts focused on the one remaining man and the chances that he had somehow survived this long in such brutal winter conditions. Search leader George Smith arrived at Chimney Pond at about 10 p.m. and made the call: There would be no attempt to reach Tom that night in the still-volatile winter conditions. Based on Paul's description of Tom's circumstance when he last saw him, there was little doubt that Tom had not survived for long in the continued deep freeze. Instead, rescue forces from the Maine Warden Service, Eastern Mountain Sports, and the Appalachian Mountain Club would meet in the morning to attempt to reach the bivouac ledge that the five recovering men had described.

At 7:30 a.m. on February 2, the mobilization began. Four rescue units moved out, and the Eastern Mountain Sports team led by Rick Wilcox was the first to reach the bivouac ledge at about noon. Here they found just what they expected: the frozen body of Tom Keddy, who had perished in the extreme cold. He hung by the rope around his waist that had kept him secured to the ledge for two nights, eight feet below the bivouac ledge.

Reaching the body was the easy part, it turned out—actually evacuating Tom would be much more challenging. The team secured the body in place and marked its position to allow them to return when the weather improved.

The storm, however, refused to abate. Temperatures held steady at twenty-five to thirty-five degrees below zero, made even colder by sixty-mile-per-hour winds and gusts of up to one hundred miles per hour. After the first effort, Park Director Buzz Caverly told a reporter from United Press International (UPI) that no further attempt to bring the body down from the mountain could be made until the wind subsided. "The rescue workers are pretty near exhaustion themselves," he said. "We can't risk sending them down that ledge on a rope to get the boy's body until those winds stop howling like that."

On Monday, February 5, UPI reported that officials still said sending a recovery team up Katahdin to retrieve the body remained "too dangerous to attempt."

"Those winds up there are murderous right now," an unnamed park ranger told the UPI reporter. "But as soon as we can see a warm front coming in we'll start to organize the rescue units again."

When the winds calmed at last on Wednesday, February 6, technical climbing teams from Baxter State Park and the Appalachian Mountain Club made their way up Katahdin to the ledge that held Tom's body. They carried him down to Chimney Pond, where a helicopter waited to fly his remains to Millinocket, and the dramatic last chapter of Tom's life came to a close nearly a week after it began.

For the rest of the climbing party, recovery meant a long convalescence, as the AAC report noted in detail.

DiBello was the most gravely injured of the five survivors, with badly frozen feet, subsequently losing one thumb, one foot and part of the other foot. In addition, he sustained varying degrees of frostbite on his face and hands. Most noses were discolored and swollen greatly, with ears, necks, cheeks, and eyes affected. Cohen's toes were in bad condition and he was on crutches for several weeks. George had one hand in bad shape, while Dinsmore required some skin grafting on his fingers. Proudman was released to home, having sustained only minor injury.

Bob went home five days after he arrived at the hospital, but Mike, Doug, and Page remained there for several weeks. Paul's recovery was the longest, requiring eight months in the hospital as doctors did their best to curtail the need for amputations.

Paul made the best of his situation in the ensuing years, however. While he required considerable additional surgery and eventually lost the rest of his remaining foot, a 1984 feature story in *Skiing* magazine detailed his success as a world-champion skier, winning medals in the 1982 Alpine World Championship for the Disabled while skiing on two prosthetic legs.

In fact, all of the surviving members of this expedition made the most of their lives. Bob took a position on the staff of the Appalachian Trail Conservancy, becoming its Director of Conservation Operations in 1981 and serving in this position for more than thirty-six years. Doug founded a company that built energy-efficient homes in New Hampshire, and Page became a veterinarian and conducted research on large-animal diseases at Colorado State University. Michael Cohen went into education in western Maine.

The realizations about what went wrong with this winter climbing expedition have become part of the record of the incident, providing plenty to chew on in the ensuing years.

The AAC ranked this incident as "preventable," listing a number of precautions the climbers could have taken to avoid the predicament in which they found themselves. The most obvious, of course, was the need for more complete weather forecast information before venturing into the Maine wilderness in the dead of winter. Radio signals were notoriously unreliable at Roaring Brook Camp in the 1970s, and they deteriorated completely the farther hikers and climbers made their way into the park. This situation is far less likely in today's WiFi-driven world, though many parks across the country are ambivalent about bringing cellular and data technologies into the backcountry.

The AAC report makes other statements about steps the expedition could have taken to prevent this tragedy, but only one of these stands out as especially useful to future climbers: the need to carry additional gear to be better prepared for the potential of an unexpected bivouac. With no sleeping roll, additional warm clothing, extra food provisions, a method of starting a fire, or emergency shelter, the six men found themselves unable to maintain a safe body temperature during the long night.

Writer Mel Allen came to this conclusion:

They say there will always be traces of guilt in having left, yet they acknowledge there was nothing else they could have done. . . . They are the survivors of a night without heroes, though surviving that storm may be heroic enough; for the storm cut short all choices but the final one, between life and death—choices for which no rules exist, not for them, not for any of us on mountains of our own, in storms we cannot foresee, storms that catch us with no warning.

CHAPTER 8

The Elderly Man and His Friend

THE PROFILE IN THE SUMMER 1974 ISSUE OF *VERMONT LIFE* MAG-
azine told glowing tales of the wilderness adventures of Augustus
Aldrich, who at eighty-six years of age still roamed the backcountry trails of New England's most spectacular areas.

Augustus, who came from Weathersfield, Vermont, had never
stopped to consider his age as he took on physical challenges that
people half his age would find daunting. He was about five feet
tall and a "104-pound bundle of rawhide and granite," according
to Thomas H. Borden of *Vermont Life*. Borden's piece focused on
a climb up Terrible Mountain in Vermont's Windsor County, a
peak that tops out at 2,694 feet, on which Augustus served as
an energetic guide to Borden, his wife, and his nine-year-old
daughter.

"I suppose the reason that my body can do what my mind
wants it to at my age is that I've worked in farming all my life,"
Augustus told Borden after he led the group up Terrible Mountain handily, climbing a forty-foot spruce tree at the summit for
the fun of it. "It's been hard work, awfully hard, but I can't com-
plain because it's what I enjoy the most."

Over decades of climbing—including his claim that he was
the first to take the 1,576 stairs to the top of the Empire State
Building—Augustus had developed some fairly quirky habits,

things no mere mortal would consider. He carried no water on hikes, telling the Bordens, "I used to carry water, but as I grew older, it grew heavier. Now I've trained myself to where I don't drink at all on the trail." His lunch of choice was peanut butter on saltine crackers, something that would be virtually impossible to swallow without a few big gulps of water—yet he managed it without a struggle. With a map in hand and a compass strapped to his arm like a watch, he navigated his way up and down the mountain wearing a fishing jacket—although, Borden noted, "he seemed more in the custody of a fishing jacket than wearing it."

Augustus brought the Bordens to the summit of Terrible Mountain and back down again without mishap in the spring of 1974—but what happened next to this "elfin wisp of an old man," in Borden's words, makes one wonder about the superstitions of our grandmothers, who told us not to draw too much attention to ourselves lest we come to the notice of evil spirits. Augustus had a moment in the sun in a magazine article during the summer of 1974, and then—as far as anyone can know—never saw the sun again.

Augustus and his friend Rachel Charland, who was fifty-six and lived in Rutland, Vermont, arrived at Baxter State Park on July 5 to climb to the top of Mount Katahdin. Augustus had a singular familiarity with the mountain and its collection of trails and peaks, as he had explored it on a number of occasions over his years of outdoor adventure. He was eager to share Katahdin's majesty with Rachel, and they hiked into the park via the Chimney Pond Trail on Friday morning with the goal of continuing to the mountaintop over the weekend. They camped there in anticipation of a good day's hike the following day.

When he went to the ranger cabin to check on trail conditions on the morning of July 6, however, Augustus discovered a notice on the bulletin board outside the cabin door. It seemed the summit trails were closed that day because of weather events toward the peaks.

Understandably disappointed, Augustus returned to their campsite and told Rachel of their curtailed plan. Then he made the decision to hike up one of the closed trails anyway, telling Rachel that he would take the Hamlin Ridge Trail to one of the summits. Rachel chose to heed the ranger's warning and stay in camp. As fog and rain enveloped the top of Katahdin and Rachel waited into the late afternoon for Augustus to return, she realized that he had been gone far too long.

By evening, Rachel told the ranger at Chimney Pond of Augustus's hike, and that he had not returned as he was scheduled to do. Once the ranger heard that an eighty-six-year-old man might be in distress on the mountain, he radioed for assistance and the search-and-rescue mission began. Professionals including park rangers, game wardens, and deputy sheriffs from Piscataquis County led volunteers in canvassing the areas on and around Mount Katahdin.

The searchers thought they were about to get an early break in their mission when a police dog followed Augustus's scent three-quarters of a mile to Blueberry Knoll even on the rain-soaked trail. "But searchers scouring that area found no trace of the missing man," the *Bangor Daily News* reported.

The search lengthened into the night and the next day, and one day followed another, and another. By the third day, law enforcement officials began to consider the outside chance that some form of foul play was involved. People usually do not vanish into the wilderness without a single shred of evidence—even though we've seen stories of several people who did so in this book. In most cases, they leave clues or some sort of trail: clothing fibers, footprints, or discarded packaging from food they carried.

Adding to the belief that something else might be afoot was Rachel's description of a letter Augustus had carried with him, apparently one he had written in Vermont before leaving. "Aldrich was very insistent about mailing [it] himself from Millinocket," *Bangor Daily News* reported. Rachel said that Augustus had brought the letter with him from Vermont, and that he did not tell her what it contained or to whom he had addressed it. "Several times he reportedly refused offers to mail the letter for him," *Bangor Daily News* continued.

This hint of a mystery quickly dissipated, however, as officers inquired with Augustus's cousin, William Wood, with whom he lived in Weathersfield. Wood told *Bangor Daily News*, "I'd think knowing Augustus that he must have had some friend he wanted to surprise, say something like, 'Hello, I'm up on top of Katahdin.'"

An even stranger report suggested that Augustus had applied for a ranger position at Baxter State Park and had been rejected because of his age, a story that some attempted to connect with his disappearance. Park Director Buzz Caverly dismissed this report by going back through his files of applications for the last twelve months and finding no form from Augustus Aldrich.

With none of these ideas turning into solid leads, the search in the park continued. By now the operation had grown to include at least eighty volunteers.

"It's Director out there and [make] no mistake," a ranger told the *Bennington Banner*, Aldrich's hometown paper, toward the end of the day on July 11, the sixth fruitless search day. "Two hundred thousand acres of wilderness is nothing to take lightly."

Park Director Buzz Caverly could only speculate about what had happened to Augustus. "It's quite difficult to conceive that he could make it up over the mountain after a rainstorm blew up, and at his age," he said to the *Banner*. "It's my personal feeling he's probably lying somewhere in the basin. . . . People persist in underestimating the mountain. It's that simple."

A Good Heart Gives Out

When word reached land planner Hollister Kent in Norwich, Vermont, that his friend Augustus Aldrich was missing, he did not hesitate for a moment to join the search.

Kent, fifty-six, was a senior partner at Planners Collaborative of Norwich and Syracuse, New York. He had applied his city- and town-planning skills to projects from Burlington, Vermont, to Brasilia, Brazil, including a period as director of town planning for Kitimat, British Columbia. Kent had provided plans for a proposed city in Venezuela and governmental centers in Puerto Rico, and a reworking of the design for Perth Central City in Australia. His reputation for giving back to his community ran deep—he served as an adjunct professor at Dartmouth College, teaching town and city planning, and as a staff director for the Institute on Man and Science in Rensselaerville, New York. With all of this activity, he also found the time to raise three sons and two daughters with his wife, Edith, and enjoy two grandchildren as well.

Knowing that his friend Augustus was in trouble, Kent dropped everything and set out for Baxter State Park to join the search. He arrived at Roaring Brook on the morning of July 9 and joined a search party on its way up the steep, rocky, three-mile trail from Roaring Brook to Chimney Pond.

They were nearing Chimney Pond when suddenly Kent stopped walking. In an instant he collapsed onto the ground. A cursory examination told the others in the party that he was not breathing and had lost consciousness.

One of the searchers turned around and broke into a run, dashing all the way down the trail to Roaring Brook to get help. A ranger and others with emergency medical training set out up the trail and reached Kent, but two hours of artificial respiration failed to revive him or even to restore his heartbeat and breathing. Search-and-rescue personnel called for a helicopter to airlift the man out of the park and take him to a hospital for more aggressive revival efforts, but bad weather grounded the helicopter.

"I sat down and cried for an hour when we lost him," a ranger at Roaring Brook told writer Kathleen Palm at the *Bennington Banner*.

Nary a Trace

Piling one tragedy on another with Hollister Kent's death did not change the facts of the situation: Aldrich was still missing, and not a single clue had surfaced.

"All the trails on the mountain have been covered several times but the searchers have seen no trace of anything," a park spokesperson told the *Bennington Banner* on Thursday, July 11. Twenty rangers and wardens and as many as sixty volunteers continued to canvass the areas around trails all over Katahdin, but they discovered no new clues. Even a day of sunny weather turned out to be no help, as strong winds made it difficult for helicopters to fly through areas above and around the mountain.

After a week without a single sign of Augustus, officials brought the search to a close at sunset on Friday, July 12. To this day, no trace of Augustus Aldrich ever came to light.

"Eventually, after all the leads have been followed through and everything humanly possible has been done in making the search itself, a search winds down," wrote Eric Wight in his book, *Life and Death in the North Woods.* "Yet an unsolved case always remains open, even though the search has been suspended."

There's no way to know what exactly transpired to take this wiry little man's life, but the *Vermont Life* story provides a sliver of a clue. On the way home in the car from the hike up Terrible Mountain, Augustus told Borden's daughter, Sarah, "Sorry I didn't stand on my head for you at the end of the hike. I always used to, but the last couple of years I find it makes me a little dizzy. I even have to be careful when I'm under the tractor making repairs. I have to make certain I'm not pointed downhill."

Might a spell of lightheadedness or even vertigo have been the cause of his disappearance? Did he lose his footing on the jagged trail up Katahdin and tumble down into the basin, becoming hidden in the thick understory?

Perhaps someday the remains of this man will come to light, just as Roger Hildreth's skeleton did long after the search for him ended, and as the missing Piper Cruiser revealed itself twelve years after it went down. In the interim, however, Wight makes an excellent point at the end of his account of the search: "Gus Aldrich is still somewhere on Mount Katahdin, and I suspect that there is where he wants to be."

CHAPTER 9

A Sliding Slab of Snow

THOSE OF US WHO DREAD THE COMING OF WINTER FIND IT HARD to understand the lure of frigid-weather sport, the enticement that drives adventurous souls to venture into the cold for fun. Winter hikers and ice climbers find a delight in conquering slippery surfaces, traversing deep drifts, and placing the first footprints on pristine paths blanketed with new-fallen snow that simply does not attract everyone—and perhaps this in itself is part of the attraction. Visitors to Mount Katahdin in the dim days of January and February can find that they have the entire mountain to themselves, a completely different experience from sharing the trails with hundreds of other hikers on a summer day.

When Bob Esser, Ken Levanway, and Steve Hilt, all from Troy, New York; Rick Cumm from Ravena, New York; and Peter Cochetti of Albany, New York, arrived at Baxter State Park on February 5, 1984, for five days of hiking and climbing, they were well prepared for what they knew they would encounter on Mount Katahdin in the frozen season. Bob led the party, and he and Ken returned for their second winter expedition, the first having occurred four years earlier, so they knew exactly what to expect from outdoor technical climbing in Katahdin's snow- and ice-encrusted gullies and on its granite walls. Rick, Peter, and Steve shared their eagerness to scale the mountain, and brought plenty of winter climbing experience to the prospect of taking on Katahdin. They all had planned this trip for the previous six months, including many meetings and research, and they had out-fitted themselves appropriately with everything they would need to scale the mountain: snowshoes, skis, winter mountain boots, sleeping bags rated for subzero temperatures, sunglasses, packs, matches in waterproof packaging, enough food for the entire trip, maps, a compass, an ice ax and crampons for each person, helmets, flashlights, and a rope for each pair of climbers. The park also required them to submit certifications of their physical fitness, as well as proof of the group leader's training and experience. They knew this would be an adventure they would remember for many years to come.

The five men, all in their twenties, qualified easily for the required permit to go into the Katahdin wilderness in mid-winter. They spent the first two days of their Baxter visit skiing and hiking in sixteen miles from the nearest road to Chimney Pond Camp, and established their camp in the cabin there on the afternoon of the second day. In the morning, they chose a fairly easy climb for such experienced outdoorsmen: they ascended the Chimney, a nearly straight vertical rise that gives summer climbers a stren-uous scramble to Chimney Peak, the smaller, sharp peak on the way to Pamola Peak, but doesn't require rock climbing equipment. It can be a technical climb in winter, however, albeit not the most difficult one on the mountain. A run up Chimney provided a good warm-up climb for the young men from New York before they tackled the gullies they had come to acquire.

Katahdin already had five feet of snow by their early February expedition. During the climb, the men made a point of observing the snow conditions in anticipation of a tougher technical route the next day. They finished the Chimney fairly early in the day, so Bob, Ken, and Rick took on a short technical climb on the Pamola ice cliff, while Peter and Steve gathered food and water for the cabin and explored the area close to camp on skis. By day's end, as they gathered in the cabin around the wood stove to make plans for the next day, Bob, Ken, and Rick said that they would get up early to climb Cilley-Barber, a 2,500-foot snow and ice gully that leads to Knife Edge and tops out near Baxter Peak. Peter and Steve decided they would head for Baxter Peak up what they called the "tourist route," the Cathedral Trail—a very steep, rocky trail that serves as a challenging hiking route in spring, summer, and fall, and becomes even more strenuous in winter.

At 6 a.m. the next day, Bob, Ken, and Rick set out for Cilley-Barber, but once they arrived at the bottom of the gully, they decided that the high winds and deep-freeze temperatures made this climb too hazardous for their comfort. They returned to the cabin by 8 a.m. and found Peter and Steve preparing for their hike up the Cathedral Trail. Not wishing to spend the rest of the morning hanging around camp, the three earlier risers decided to join Peter and Steve "just to get out," and they all set out together in the direction of First Cathedral, a huge formation of jagged boulders that forms a promontory near Baxter Peak.

"We followed the trail markers, rotating breaking trail," Peter later explained to the Associated Press (AP). All of the men had agreed the day before that the snow appeared to be stable, and now, with their ski masks and goggles in place, none of them could see enough to believe that their first analysis was anything but correct.

They hadn't been on the trail more than fifteen or twenty minutes and were about fifty feet up the trail from the base, according to Peter's account to the AP, when they all suddenly felt the impact of a wall of snow rushing down the mountain.

"When the snow knocked him on his back, [Peter] was completely covered, and could only sense that he was falling head-first down the mountain on his back," the chronicle of the American Alpine Club reports. "He fell for a long time and then hit something on his back which was very hard and was absorbed by the pack he was wearing."

When Peter finally came to rest, he found himself hemmed in on all sides by heavy snow—including over his head. He became instantly aware that he could not breathe or see. Checking his limbs, he discovered that he could move his right hand, so he wiggled it hard until he freed his arm and could begin to dig out.

"He was clawing with all he was worth," said the report, "and finally was able to remove both arms, and then able to open airways to his mouth."

Peter dug snow away from his face as fast as he could, and soon found that he was only about a foot and a half under the snow. The more he dug, the more he freed his body until he finally managed to dig himself out altogether. He checked his arms, legs, and ribs as he stood up, found with relief that he had no broken bones, and immediately whirled around to find his friends.

Peter shouted, and Rick answered, his head sticking out of the snow. Peter ran to him and pulled off his face mask, and Rick immediately started yelling, "There's someone beneath me. Get him out!"

If one of the men had been completely buried in the snow, every second could mean oxygen deprivation and eventual suffocation. Peter quickly dug the snow out from around Rick's face to ease his breathing, and then began digging where Rick said he could feel another person under him. Five minutes of scratching away at the snow with his gloves and boots made little headway, however. Peter realized that to be effective at freeing anyone else, he had to get a shovel. He glanced at his watch—it was a few minutes before 10 a.m. Peter got to his feet and ran back to the ranger's cabin for tools and additional help.

When Ranger Charlie Kenney heard what was happening on the mountain, he gave Peter a shovel and sent him back up to the scene of the avalanche while he called park headquarters. In minutes Kenney was on his way toward First Cathedral with another shovel, an ice ax, and other emergency gear.

By the time Kenney reached Peter, he found that he had already managed to find and clear the snow from the heads of all four of the other climbers. Rick and Bob had survived the ordeal, but Ken and Steve, the two who were buried farther down, had both stopped breathing. Ranger Kenney and Peter attempted CPR on both men, but they could not restore breathing or a heartbeat. Ken Levanway and Steve Hilt had perished in the avalanche.

Now Peter and Kenney focused on removing Bob and Rick from the snow. "The avalanche had set up very fast and, consequently, the snow was hard packed, making it extremely difficult to shovel Esser and Cumm out," the AAC report noted. Peter and the ranger dug as hard and as fast as they could, and they managed to free both men from the heavy snow after considerable time. By now, Bob was barely breathing. Peter and Ranger Kenney administered CPR, and to their relief, they were successful in reviving Bob. By now, however, hypothermia had become a potential factor with two men incapacitated by snow pack and broken bones. Peter and Ranger Kenney performed first aid, packed extra clothing around the two men to keep them as warm as possible in the five-below-zero cold, and recognized that the two climbers had sustained broken bones and other injuries. They would need assistance to bring them off the mountain and evacuate them to the hospital in Millinocket, some twenty miles away.

It seemed like an eternity passed during the digging, but by the time Peter and the ranger had freed Bob and Rick, reinforcements had arrived to help. Ranger Robert Howes was the first to reach the victims, as he had been involved in trail work not far from Chimney Pond Camp. Al Cooper, the owner of Katahdin Lake Camps, came down the trail next, with Paul Rumney, a forest technician, with him. Soon support came from Northern Timber Cruisers, the snowmobile and cross-country ski club in Millinocket; Dirigo Search and Rescue Team out of Orono, Maine; and other park personnel, volunteers, and their family members. This influx of assistance gave Peter and Ranger Kenney the opportunity to finish digging out Steve and Ken, so they could be evacuated after Bob and Rick were safe.

First the rescuers carried Bob and Rick into Chimney Pond Camp, where they wrapped them in warm blankets and "attempted to get something warm to drink into them," the report noted. Later in the afternoon, a helicopter arrived to take Bob, Rick, and Peter to Millinocket Regional Hospital. Once the three survivors of the avalanche were on their way, the remaining crew assembled snowmobiles and tote sleds to take the bodies of Steve and Ken down Chimney Pond Trail and out of the park.

"Night had fallen by the time a team of a dozen volunteers and park rescuers brought the bodies of Levanway and Hilt down a twenty-mile trail by snowmobile," reported Peter Jackson of the Associated Press. "They were taken to a funeral home in Millinocket."

The following day, United Press International reported that the injured climbers were in "stable" condition at Millinocket Regional Hospital. Peter had been checked over by the emergency room staff and released.

"They were sore from head to foot. Both of them were in severe pain," emergency medical technician Jon C. Crawford told the reporter.

Bob and Rick both had broken legs, but they requested that no further information be released to the public. "They prefer not to release anything at this time and I think that's understandable," hospital spokesperson James Morrissey told the media. "It's a tragedy. No one can appreciate what they've gone through."

Understanding an Avalanche

Removing the victims from the scene was only the beginning of the job, as far as Park Director Buzz Caverly was concerned. He wanted the answer to a larger question: Could the climbers—and the park staff—have missed the signs of an impending avalanche?

Caverly engaged Kevin Slater, a graduate student from the University of Maine with considerable technical climbing experience, to test and analyze the snow pack.

Slater determined that the avalanche was a "delayed slab response," a buildup of layers that did not adhere firmly to one another. Snow from earlier in the winter formed the initial layer at the bottom, which was followed by rain and then a plunge of temperature that froze the bottom layer into ice. Granulated snow fell after that, the kind of snow that crystallizes and does not adhere firmly to layers above or below it. Just a few days before this climbing party arrived, heavy, wet snow—about two feet of it—fell and covered the granulated snow. This wet snow turned into slab about fifty feet square, and as it balanced precariously in place on a steep angle, the five climbers began to cross it.

"It is Kevin's opinion that the weight of the climbers hiking over that area is what triggered the avalanche," wrote Caverly, who authored the AAC report. "He clearly pointed out, though, that there was no way that the climbers could have known that that situation existed. Even he or other rangers who might have been in the area wouldn't have known they were in the same situation. It was a case of those people not doing anything wrong, unaware of what was happening beforehand, but being caught in the wrong place at the wrong time."

Knowing the condition of the snow on Katahdin in that one area, Slater conducted additional testing and determined that "there were several other potential avalanches just waiting to be triggered." The park acted quickly to restrict climbing to areas of exposed rock and solid ice until conditions improved, so there would be no other lives lost that winter.

The 1984 avalanche event was the only case in which someone died on Katahdin because of an unexpected wall of rushing snow. While avalanches are common here, especially on Cathedral Trail, in Cilley-Barber gully, and on Saddle Trail and the Chimney, visitors who intend to hike, climb, or ski Katahdin in winter are careful to check with rangers about weather and snow conditions before venturing out. The most experienced winter sports enthusiasts know the signs of an impending avalanche, but—as we saw in 1984—not every avalanche provides clues, and even highly skilled technical climbers may be unaware of the hazardous conditions hidden under several feet of new snowfall.

CHAPTER 10

Over the Knife Edge

MOST VISITORS TO MOUNT KATAHDIN WOULD AGREE THAT IF they had to choose one route that served as a "signature" hike for the park—one that provided the ultimate, unforgettable Baxter State Park experience—it would be the Knife Edge.

This mile-long pathway along the top edge of the mountain between Baxter Peak and Pamola Peak, a good 2,500 feet above Chimney Pond, gives hikers the most thrilling views of the Longfellow Mountains throughout the park, but this is only a fraction of the trail's appeal. Knife Edge furnishes the bravest hikers with the gasp-inducing experience of balancing on a narrow granite ribbon of rock about three feet wide, with total exposure on all sides and no railings or handholds of any kind.

"The drop from either side is dizzying," wrote Ranger Steven Tetreault in his book, *The Bear Dogs of Katahdin: And Other Recollections of a Baxter State Park Ranger*. "The trail is dangerous in high winds and poor weather conditions."

On either side of the slender trail, long slopes of jagged granite boulders reach up toward the top of the mountain, making a sudden fall not so much a precipitous drop for the unfortunate hiker, but a body roll punctuated by blow after blow from the unforgiving, serrated rocks.

This may sound like a deathtrap rather than a peak experience (pun intended), but the fact is that only two people have died in a fall from Knife Edge since the park began keeping death records in 1926. One of these, fifty-seven-year-old Richard Smith Jr. actually fell from the trail after experiencing a heart attack during his hike in July 1998, which may or may not have been triggered by the trail's scary precariousness.

The other is the kind of tragedy that becomes the stuff of nightmares.

Steve Tetreault was a rookie ranger in the summer of 1986, just beginning to understand the responsibilities his position required. At twenty-one years old, he lived in the cabin at Togue Pond, where he worked to rehabilitate an area that had been overused and "civilized," bringing it back to its natural state. As staff throughout Baxter State Park has always been limited, Steve often received calls to do things other than his assigned duties. This sunny Sunday in August brought him a new experience, one he had not really considered when he signed on to be a ranger.

The radio in Steve's truck—the only radio he had, so he kept it on whenever he was on duty—suddenly erupted with a call from Unit 12, the ranger on mountain patrol. Radio calls usually had to do with campground reservations and other mundane issues, but this one had a special urgency.

"Esther," the ranger said, addressing Esther Hendrickson, the campground ranger at Chimney Pond, "I think someone just fell off your Knife Edge."

Nothing gets the attention of every ranger like a notice that someone may be in trouble in the park. Steve dropped what he was doing to listen closely to the transmission.

Details came in pieces. Steve learned that a sixteen-year-old boy, part of a group of thirteen adults and teens, had been in the process of hiking from Chimney Pond up the Cathedral Trail to Baxter Peak, and then across the Knife Edge and down the Dudley Trail. They had reached the Knife Edge and crossed at least half of the mile-long trail when three of the boys left the marked route to do what others had attempted in the past: They decided to explore what they thought was a "shortcut," a side trail leading down from South Peak at the Knife Edge's midpoint.

Derek Quiet, sixteen, of Dover-Foxcroft, joined Lance Johnson, who was eighteen and from Sangerville, and Wayne Grant, a seventeen-year-old also from Dover-Foxcroft, in attempting to find a faster route back to Chimney Pond. Derek and other members of the larger party had climbed Katahdin before, so they felt the confidence that often comes with familiarity, certain that they knew the trail well enough to avoid the built-in pitfalls of Maine's highest mountain.

They followed the faint path down the side of the mountain for a good five hundred feet until they reached the headwall, a sheer ledge from which the boys would need technical gear to climb down. They hadn't bargained for this, however—they didn't have the required ropes, pitons, and other specialized equipment.

"The descent to Chimney Pond from this point looks possible to the untrained eye," Tetreault wrote. "At first, the drops are easy to handle and you think you can continue down—until you reach a drop that can only be navigated with ropes and rock climbing gear. You decide to turn around and go back up but find you can't climb up what you just came down. You're trapped."

Twenty-three years earlier, Margaret Ivusic made the same error, attempting what appeared to be an easy route back to camp and finding herself hopelessly stuck at the top of a precipitous drop, and at the bottom of a field of rotten rock, prone to crumbling underfoot. She perished from exposure overnight. Now Derek, Lance, and Wayne realized that they, too, could be trapped on the mountainside if they didn't turn back right away.

Turning, however, knocked Derek off balance. In the time it takes for a young man to suck in his breath in a gasp, Derek dropped over the headwall.

He slid about six feet, caught himself on a rock, and attempted to stand and steady himself. Looking around him, he knew that he had gone too far—he could not make his way back up the slab he had just slid down, and the sheer rock face below him was too steep to proceed any farther.

Derek called to his friends, asking them to get help. They had just turned away to start back up the path to the top when Derek's scream shattered the backcountry silence. The rocks under his feet broke apart and skittered away. Derek lost his footing and plunged down the mountainside, still screaming twice more as he fell.

"From that point, [the other two boys] did not see him anymore," Chief Ranger Chris Drew told the *Bangor Daily News* later that day.

"They didn't know how far he fell or how badly he was hurt—or, if he had even survived," Tetreault wrote. "They raced back to Baxter Peak."

The two boys, now terrified for their friend, found park patrol member Jayson Kay, who sent out the Unit 12 message to all the rangers in the park. By the time the boys reached the ranger, it was about 2 p.m., an hour after Derek had slipped away over the ledge.

South district Ranger Bob Howes described to *Bangor Daily News* the area where Derek fell as "very rocky, steep, jagged, with a lot of loose, rotten rock. It's no place for free-climbing without protection or ropes."

Mobilizing for Recovery

Reaching Derek's position would take some time. No marked trails led directly to the area where the boy's body came to rest, so getting there required rangers to go all the way around Chimney Pond—a hike that would take at least thirty minutes—and then make their way up gullies through thick scrub brush, fallen rock, and the thick, stunted vegetation called krummholz that lives in this kind of subalpine landscape. When the rangers reached the bottom of the glacial cirque that flanks Chimney Pond, they needed to work their way up a wall of rock that got steeper as the team moved upward, a route used regularly by rock climbers to reach the area that requires technical gear.

After all this hiking in progressively more challenging conditions, the rangers would reach the cliffs that rose straight up for hundreds of feet. "A volunteer completed this bushwhack and reached a point where he could see through binoculars the result of the hiker's fall," Tetreault said in his book. "There was no doubt that this rescue was going to be a search and recovery—nobody was alive to be rescued."

Steve Tetreault told me firsthand by phone in February 2018 about what happened next on Katahdin after the rangers in the area got the call from Unit 12.

"Everyone in striking distance, you stop and wait to see if you can help," he said. "Once they determined that he was not alive, there was no need to endanger anyone else in trying to rescue him."

With this fact confirmed, Howes decided that they would begin the recovery process in the morning, rather than attempt it late in the day and have it continue into the evening and after dark. In the interim, he contacted the 112th Medevac team of the Army National Guard to request a helicopter to transport the body out of the park the following day, once the rangers and volunteers had removed it from the mountain. The National Guard helicopter brought in members of the Dirigo Search and Rescue Team from Orono. At the same time, a helicopter from Brunswick Naval Air Station brought in members of the Wilderness Search and Rescue from Waterville and Portland, and two other search-and-rescue teams from Lincoln and Camden arrived as well. The combined crews included nearly fifty people, and secretaries from Baxter State Park kept them all fed with continuous meal service throughout the search and recovery process.

Tetreault and his supervisor, Ranger Bernard Crabtree, spent the rest of the afternoon preparing to hike into Chimney Pond at dawn. Another ranger, Lester Kenway, organized his trail crew to bring out the body on a litter, a process that would require several people to carry the stretcher back through the same scrub, rock, and krummholz they had passed through to reach Derek. The challenges of the route and the weight of the litter over so much terrain would require frequent changeovers from one crew to another, so Howes called for a substantial crew of search-and-rescue volunteers who could spell one another on the trail.

"The plan was to get the hiker's body down to Roaring Brook by nightfall," Tetreault wrote, "but the weather was not cooperating."

Clouds enshrouded the top 2,500 feet of the mountain, all the way down to Chimney Pond, and the damp, clammy cold felt like winter in the middle of August. Fog punctuated by moments of sunlight made the going slower than the crews had anticipated, and a helicopter evacuation in these conditions would be problematic at best.

Still, the crews made their way carefully up the congested trail. Tetreault found himself close behind Howes as they inched up the gullies beyond Chimney Pond. Sudden bands of dense cloud cover blocked his view of Howes, making it altogether too easy to move off in the wrong direction and find himself alone on a treacherous stretch of jagged rock. He pulled out his walkie-talkie and let Howes know that he had lost visual contact, and the older ranger talked him back onto the proper route.

Howes turned to him at a particularly tricky portion of the trail and said, "So, you want to be a ranger?"

"I knew what he meant," Tetreault told me. "He meant, 'You're the one who has to go help. You're going to see people who fall, who get hurt. This is part of the life of a ranger, and you have to have the ability to deal with that.'"

Indeed, this mission had become particularly difficult. Lester Kenway's team of search-and-rescue professionals "had been trying all morning to reach the body," Tetreault wrote. "The hiker's body was still up high where ropes and pitons were needed to get up and down the mountainside." The wind, cold, cloying damp, and difficult climbing took their toll on the recovery teams, and Howes began to see the early effects of hypothermia in some of the men.

Howes knew that he could not sanction a mission that put the lives of the rescuers at risk. He discussed the matter by radio with Chris Drew, chief ranger, who told him that it was up to him to use his best judgment about continuing the operation in such an environment. The day's weather report, Drew told him, called for worsening conditions for the rest of the day, making the success of the mission even more doubtful—but the clouds would clear the following day, making it much more likely that the crews could actually reach the body and bring it out of the park.

In the meantime, the Dirigo team had reached the body. Kevin Slater, one of the team members, explained the situation to Mary Anne Lagasse of the *Bangor Daily News*: He said that Derek's body had been found about a thousand feet down from Knife Edge, in Cilley-Barber gully, "a technical climb and one of the longest and steepest ice routes on Mount Katahdin."

Park Director Buzz Caverly told the media that Derek had fallen a total of about five hundred feet. "The team that went up estimated he dropped straight about 100 feet and then crashed and rolled another 400 feet," he said.

"We had to rappel to get the body down. That is how steep it was," Slater told the *Bangor Daily News.* The team had moved the body down about nine hundred feet, rappelling three times down three-hundred-foot drops. They then encountered "loose shale rock at very steep angles," which slowed the evacuation substantially. When a driving rain began to fall in the early afternoon with no signs of stopping, team leaders agreed that continuing to work was too great a risk to the search-and-rescue teams.

They had secured the body in an opaque orange bag that would protect it from the weather and any other interference, and make it easier to spot when they returned the following day to transport it off the mountain. With this important task completed, Howes called for all personnel to turn back to Chimney Pond Camp, where most of them would stay at the ranger's camp or the bunkhouse overnight with the plan of completing the mission the next morning.

Caverly also spoke with the media, explaining that if the weather did not improve as expected and it became impossible to bring a helicopter to Chimney Pond Camp, rescue teams would have to carry Derek's body out of the park on a stretcher. The 3.3-mile hike would require crews to relieve one another repeatedly, as the trail was a "mean lug, rocky, rough, narrow trails, with a trench on one side and high ground on the other side, steep downgrade, rocks, boulders, stumps, roots, rough going and slippery traveling—all of the things you don't want on a stretcher carry."

Tetreault decided to return to his own cabin on Togue Pond, but in the morning, he discovered that his role in the mission had changed. Howes had assigned him to fly into Chimney Pond with the National Guard crew on their helicopter, and informed him that he would fly out with them as well, to represent the park when the helicopter flew Derek's body out to Millinocket. At the airport, he would meet Derek's parents and deliver their son's body to them.

On Tuesday morning, the weather improved significantly and crews numbering more than twenty individuals brought the boy's body off the mountain to the waiting helicopter at Chimney Pond. This involved one recovery team to lower the body down the steep pitches to the litter team, which would carry him down a portion of the mountain that did not require technical gear.

Caverly described this as "a tough row to hoe, but they [the rescuers] all held up well. . . . The mission was accomplished because of a lot of hard work, sweat and risk to the people who are working in terrain like that. . . . They were dealing with loose shale rock as well as steep downgrades. It was a very tough job today. The conditions were far from ideal. Just climbing that with a small pack on your back, there is a risk involved. You could step on a set of rocks and slide. Visualize that same situation with a stretcher and five people coming down on an incline. The risk for injury is there. We take all the precautions we can under those circumstances. That is why we don't have any injuries as the result of this operation. It accounts for the long period of time it takes to move a stretcher off [the mountain]."

The director's tone and detailed account of the recovery's potential hazards came in response to criticism from some individuals among the general public that the retrieval of the body should have gone more quickly. The perception that delays made a bad situation worse for the grieving family became an issue during the two days of attempted recovery.

"Caverly said some people had the impression 'that guy is up on the side of the mountain. Why don't they lug him down? It's not that simple,'" the *Bangor Daily News* reported. "He said he would like to take everyone to Chimney Pond and show them what the terrain was like." Two other emergencies in the park during the same time frame—one with a Boy Scout at Chimney Pond, and another on Horse Mountain—resulted in crises averted by attentive rangers. "We had the potential for more problems," he said, but alert staff members in other parts of the park kept these situations from turning into rescue operations.

Finally, on Tuesday afternoon, it was time to bring Derek out of the park and return him to his family.

"I got in the 'copter, and Derek was loaded in front of me," Tetreault told me. "I thought, 'This is an actual person here.' He thought he was taking a shortcut, he didn't think he was going to fall, but the rocks under his feet gave way. He thought, 'It's a mountain, it's hard, it's granite.' He didn't think he'd just fall off."

He admitted to feeling some trepidation as the crew placed the body into the helicopter. "I remember feeling strange that I was that close to death," he said. "Lester had told me what he looked like." But the real sense of dread came from the moment when he would face the boy's parents.

"As the helicopter approached, I could see two vehicles parked and four people standing nearby, looking ever so small from up high," he said. "One vehicle was a hearse, one a sedan. Two people looked to be from a local funeral home. There was no doubt who the other two people were. . . . I could see their sadness and disbelief. I could see their shoulders were slumped in grief."

The funeral directors stepped forward first and accepted the body, and there was no opportunity for Tetreault to speak to the parents. They turned away as soon as the business of taking charge of their son's body was completed.

"I don't think I could have said anything to comfort them," he said. "'Sorry for your loss' doesn't quite cut it in a situation like that."

Later that afternoon, Tetreault had the opportunity to consider all that had happened over the last two days, and to think again about the question Howes had asked him on the mountain. "I was thinking that I didn't like this part of my job at all," he wrote. "The kid was just five years younger than I was. . . . I couldn't help thinking how many times I had already crossed the Knife Edge and never really felt threatened."

The day wasn't finished with Tetreault yet, however. Just as he was about to step out of the headquarters and head back to his cabin, one of the reservation clerks stopped him. She had just received a call that a family staying on Togue Pond had had a death in the family—and since there was no phone in their cabin, the news needed to be delivered to them by canoe. Togue Pond was Tetreault's jurisdiction, so he had to make the trip and break the news to the family.

Luckily, this was a much easier mission than the one he had just completed. The family took the news gracefully, and the father even offered to use his small powerboat to tow Tetreault and his canoe back across the lake, saving him "a long, hard paddle back against the wind."

It seemed like the episode had come to an end, but the death of the young man on the mountain had one more whack of surrealism left to deal to Tetreault—this one a year later, on the anniversary of the event. On the Facebook page for his book, Tetreault has posted the remarkable story of seeing a phantom of Derek—called Tommy in this account—as he returned from his own hike up Katahdin on his day off. "It was strange to see a lone hiker, a kid really, alone on a Katahdin trail so late in the day," he wrote. "No pack, no water, a white tee shirt in tatters, orange basketball shorts and only one hiking boot. Odd, indeed . . . maybe [I'd] have to help him down to Roaring Brook."

When he rounded the next turn, he expected to catch up with the boy and offer him his assistance . . . but "the trail . . . was empty. Nothing. Nothing but rock outcrops and last year's dead leaves."

He called to the boy, and "thought he heard a voice—faint and disembodied." Referring to himself in third person, Tetreault continued, "It gave him a chill but he shook it off as fatigue. . . . He shrugged his shoulders and continued down the trail. But within three steps, he felt a cold, icy chill go through him, pierce him and then surround him. . . . [H]e felt odd—peculiar—like he was being watched by something, or someone."

When he arrived at Roaring Brook, he checked with rangers there and determined that no hikers were lost on the mountain; everyone who had signed the registry earlier that day had signed back in that evening. He put the incident out of his thoughts and never breathed a word of it to anyone.

He always believed, however, that he saw Derek Quiet on the mountain on that day, one year after the boy's death, and finally committed the story to computer in 2015, twenty-eight years later. The appearance of this young man, making his way down the trail on which he never returned in life, has become a legend on

Katahdin for young rangers working in the park. In some years, on August 12, rangers say they spot a lone, disheveled teenage boy on Chimney Pond Trail, and some even hear his voice. Katahdin is far from the only mountain that may be haunted by the phantom of a young person who died too soon, but this story is among the most poignant and heartbreaking, particularly when told firsthand by those who were there when it happened.

CHAPTER 11

A Peak Bagger's Obsession

NOTHING CREATES A SENSE OF ACCOMPLISHMENT LIKE CHECK-
ing things off a list, seeing all those ticks and remembering the
pleasure and sense of triumph of completing each item. We make
lists of to-do items around the house, at work, or in our community activities, and every time we cross something off, we experience a burst of relief that this thing has been completed.

Why not apply this same sense of accomplishment to our
experiences in nature? Birders have their life lists, the tallies of
bird species they have seen in their lifetimes, sliced and diced into
continent lists, country lists, state lists, even county lists and back-
yard lists. National park enthusiasts have the list of 417 national
park units in the United States and its territories, an exciting
catalog to crisscross the country to fulfill, ticking off one park
after another and racking up hundreds of fascinating experiences.
And hikers have their peak-bagging lists, checking off each of the
mountains they climb over a certain elevation in a certain state
or region, whether it's the fifty-four mountains in Colorado over
14,000 feet, the forty-eight peaks over 4,000 feet in the Adiron-
dack Mountains of New York State, or the one hundred highest
peaks in New England.

"Peak-bagging is not an organized sport, game or athletics
in the usual sense," writes Ernest F. Imhoff, who was assistant

managing editor with the *Baltimore Sun* in the 1990s, and a committed peak bagger in his own right. "It is practiced alone or with others, hours or days away from cars and cities. Hikers begin by hiking up one mountain and enjoying the beauty of rushing waters or the quiet of the woods or the music of the birds or the physical demands of several hours walking 1,000 to 5,000 feet higher in altitude and down again. They try another mountain and another and another, the height and difficulty usually increasing. They become dedicated, hooked, then possibly obsessed. . . . They quickly learn there are lists of hills. At first these are excuses to visit secluded tops ordinarily missed. Soon, the hikers start collecting."

Jeffrey Z. Rubin, PhD, had just one peak left to climb. A hiker since childhood, he had scaled mountains around the globe including Mount Kilimanjaro, the highest mountain on the continent of Africa at 19,341 feet, and others on every continent in the world. He had also reached the tops of ninety-nine of the hundred highest peaks in New England, braving the volatile weather conditions on New Hampshire's Mount Washington at 6,289 feet—the tallest peak in the northeast—and enjoying the comparatively easy hike up Dorset Mountain in Vermont's Taconic region, the smallest on the list at 3,760 feet.

Only one mountain remained: Fort Mountain in Baxter State Park, the northernmost of the peaks, though certainly not the highest. Fort Mountain lands at number seventy-eight on the Appalachian Mountain Club's official list of the highest peaks in New England, topping out at 3,867 feet. If this number sounds like a pleasant stroll to readers who have summited peaks in the Rocky Mountains or the North Cascades, let me assure you that while Fort Mountain's actual elevation may not impress you, reaching the summit presents its own variety of challenges.

No marked trail leads up Fort Mountain. Most people who choose to summit it follow the Marston Trail to the 4,143-foot summit of neighboring North Brother Mountain, a trek that can take three to four hours in good weather—and all day if the area's frequent rains set in. From North Brother, the most practical route to Fort is the "herd path," the trail worn relatively clear by previous hikers, but one that is not maintained by the park. Hikers proceed at their own risk, following the unmarked path through spruce forest to thick krummholz and choosing as best they can from mysterious side trails that lead in a number of wrong directions. An incorrect choice can mean an exhausting bushwhack through congested forest with a persistent understory of low-growing branches and twigs, with the possibility that you may not find your way to the summit. Faint paths that look viable can lead hikers into forest that becomes impenetrable in the space of a few feet, hiding the main trail—such as it is—from view. It's easy to see how a lone hiker or even an entire hiking party could become lost on this mountainside in the space of a couple of minutes.

When finally you break free of the forest and arrive above the tree line, there are two possible summits in front of you, one of which is slightly taller than the other, though this is not obvious from the trail. Many hikers decide to climb both to be sure that they have actually summited Fort Mountain, but only one has the marker that confirms it's the taller of the two. By the time they reach the top of Fort, most hikers have spent five hours or more on the trail, especially if the weather did not cooperate and the going was slower than planned. Given the lack of trail markings; the near-certainty of taking a wrong turn or two on the herd paths; the possibility of encountering low cloud cover, fog, rain, mud, and even flowing water in the middle of the path; and blackflies, mosquitoes, and other insect pests, hikers do their best to complete their return trip in daylight.

None of this frightened Jeffrey Rubin, who at fifty-four had extensive hiking experience that had seen him through far more daunting challenges than this. He planned an excursion for the weekend of June 2, 3, and 4, 1995, with his friend Daniel Lieberfeld, a thirty-five-year-old college professor in Cambridge,

Massachusetts. (Dr. Lieberfeld cordially declined to be interviewed for this book.)

Rubin, a psychology professor at Tufts University in Cambridge, specialized in negotiations and conflict resolution and was one of the most respected professionals in his field. He earned his doctorate at Columbia University in New York City, received a prestigious Fulbright Fellowship, and built a career around negotiation and diplomacy, teaching at the Fletcher School of Law and Diplomacy at Tufts and serving as the executive director of the Program on Negotiation at Harvard Law School. He was president of the Society for the Psychological Study of Social Issues, and had spent an academic year as a senior lecturer at Tel Aviv University in Israel. He also authored, co-authored, or edited more than twenty books on conflict resolution, bargaining, and negotiation, including one on conflict within families with his wife, Carol Milligan Rubin. The *UCLA Law Review* called Rubin "one of the key theorists and founders of the modern conflict resolution field."

A hike up a fairly small mountain in Maine on a late spring day would not intimidate a man with so many accomplishments. He had already scaled all the other mountains on his list, including seventy-seven that were higher than Fort Mountain, and many that featured far more rugged terrain. Jeff and Daniel expected this weekend to be one more triumph, ending with a celebration of Jeff's one hundredth and last New England peak.

They drove up to Baxter State Park on Friday, June 2, and made camp not far from the Marston trailhead, planning to start their trek early on Saturday morning. The day began pleasantly enough, though the forecast called for rain later in the afternoon, so they made tracks up to the summit of North Brother Mountain. By the time they reached it, however, the promised rains had arrived. High winds, pelting downpour, and fog that obscured the herd paths made the going slow at best, and the longer they pushed forward in these conditions, the less Daniel wanted to go on.

After a quarter-mile of bushwhacking through what he described later as scrub that felt like barbed wire, Daniel decided he'd had enough. He told Jeff he had gone as far as he cared to—it was time to head back to camp, and perhaps try this hike again on another weekend.

Jeff, however, had no intention of turning around when he was so close to the final summit on his list. From the top of North Brother on a clear day, he would have only another hour or so to hike to the summit of Fort Mountain. Today there was no telling how long this walk above the tree line through wind and rain might take, but he knew that he could bear the discomfort for the reward of bagging his last summit.

Daniel understood his friend's determination, but he knew his own limits. He turned back and headed down the Marston Trail to dry clothes and a warm fire at their campsite, while Jeff went on alone.

Daniel reached the campsite, dried off, and made himself comfortable, and waited for his friend to return. As the last of the afternoon stretched on into evening and Jeff did not emerge from the trail, Daniel became concerned, and as the long, near-solstice evening finally gave way to night amid continued rain and whipping winds, he knew that something had gone wrong. He left the campsite and found a warden, and told him that his friend was still on the mountain.

The wardens organized a search that began at daybreak on Sunday morning, June 4. They soon discovered Jeffrey Rubin at the base of Fort Mountain. He was face down in Wassataquoik Stream, and his body was covered in bruises. This, said V. Paul Reynolds, spokesperson for the state Department of Inland Fisheries and Wildlife, indicated that he may have fallen to his death.

A helicopter arrived to carry Jeff's body to Millinocket, where the medical examiner performed an autopsy the following day. He determined that Jeff had drowned, indicating that he was still alive when he fell into the stream. "Officials theorized that Rubin became disoriented and fell," the Associated Press reported.

Had he made it to the summit? "It's possible," Park Director Buzz Caverly said to the media, "but not likely."

Colleagues, friends, and family were quick to comment on Jeff's obsession with climbing, as well as his lasting positive impact on his professional community.

Rick Mancke, interim dean at the Fletcher School of Law and Diplomacy and a hiker as well, suggested that Jeff had taken his goal of summiting the hundred peaks "a bit too seriously," according to the AP.

"He wanted to get it done. I guess he wasn't going to be diverted from that," Mancke said. "I think there's a lesson to be learned. . . . They could have waited another day. You don't really have to do it that weekend."

He recollected a conversation with Rubin about his passion for mountain climbing. "I said, 'The difference between you and me, Jeff, is you're obsessed.' And I think, unfortunately, that was true."

"He was definitely a driven person," Fletcher School colleague Sarah Thayer told the Associated Press. "He was very determined to succeed."

His family noted that Jeff died in a way that would have suited him. "He died a heroic, gallant death," his daughter, Sally Rubin, said at his funeral to more than 250 mourners. "We often talk about living life to its fullest, but my father was someone who did."

CHAPTER 12

Under Water and Rocks: Bad Luck and Hubris in the Wilderness

It's been said that a bad day fishing is better than a good day at work, but Ferdinand G. Hunter might have disagreed.

The forty-five-year-old janitor for the Bangor-Aroostook Railroad and his friend Herbert Kenney, who was sixty at the time, spent a fairly dank day on Saturday, April 28, 1945, on First Lake Matagamon in the northeastern corner of Baxter State Park, waiting for salmon to bite. In between castings and attempts to move around the lake, they battled the finicky outboard motor on Kenney's sponson canoe—that is, a canoe equipped with short "wings" that are meant to stabilize the craft and keep it from tipping over.

The motor had given the two men fits the entire day, and at 10 p.m., they found themselves in the middle of the lake with no power. Repeated attempts to start the motor failed, and one of the men gave the starter a particularly hard and wild yank.

Sponsons or no, the canoe capsized, throwing both men into water that must have hovered in the forty-five-degree range below the warmer surface.

Both men scrambled through the water and managed to get a grip on the turtled canoe, an early win in a night that could not get much worse. Now they had to find a way to turn the canoe back over—a process complicated by the ineffective sponsons—or swim for the nearest land, an island not far from where they had been thrown from the boat. They opted to swim for it.

Kenney made it to the island and crawled out of the water onto the shore. Hunter was not far behind him, but about fifty feet from the shore, he disappeared from view and did not emerge.

Chilled to the bone and shivering, a sign that hypothermia could set in at any moment, Kenney saw that he had no hope of rescuing Hunter. He had no idea where to find him in the ink-black water, and he would more than likely become too cold to function in the space of a few minutes. Kenney watched the water as some of the bedding that had been in the canoe floated toward him, and he pulled it ashore and wrapped himself in it—even wet, it worked with his remaining body heat to offer him some warmth—and he waited through the night until he could flag down a passing boat in the morning.

Sure enough, in the early light, "a man employed on the eastern drive" spotted Kenney and contacted the police. Deputy Sheriff Fred Bailey organized the effort to bring Kenney off the island and back to Patten, and then to retrieve Hunter's body. He reported to the media that Kenney was found "in a cold and exhausted condition Sunday morning," but that the stranded man was expected to make a full recovery.

Assisted by two state troopers and two game wardens, Bailey led the recovery process, finding the location of Hunter's body and using grappling hooks to lift it out of the lake. The team completed their task shortly before 1 p.m. Once it was clear that no foul play had taken place and that Kenney and Hunter had simply had an unfortunate accident, Kenney headed home to Houlton.

The Worst Day of a Life

Some people lose their lives in a park because of a fatal error, like a missed weather forecast or a knot improperly tied in a critically important rope. Some take their lives into their own hands to attempt a dangerous climb or to pit their own strength against the elements. Others do not have any idea what they will face when they wander off into the wilderness, and do not take the most basic precautions to protect themselves.

And some people just hit a spot of bad luck.

Such was the fate of Ferdinand Hunter, who believed he was in a boat reinforced against the possibility of capsizing. Perhaps Charles Marr and two unnamed companions, all of whom drowned in Trout Brook sometime in October 1967, also simply went fishing on the wrong day—but their end came so quietly that only the park, not the media, noted it in their records. A man named Frank Heath met his last day in South Branch Pond while fishing, though I can find no other information beyond that. Whether these souls did something terribly wrong or were stunned to find themselves struggling in a mountain waterway—or both—is anyone's guess.

A task as innocent as retrieving a pack led a visitor to a watery end on July 30, 1997, when thirty-eight-year-old Philip Duvall of Richmond, Virginia, fished in the stream below Little Niagara Falls on Nesowadnehunk Stream. Duvall was one of fourteen people camping together at Katahdin Stream Campground, and when he realized that he had left his pack at the top of the falls and began heading back up the stream to get it, one of his companions tossed the pack to him.

Duvall reached for the pack as it came through the air toward him, lost his balance, and fell. "The fast-moving water carried Duvall the distance to the falls, where he became lodged between two rocks, the water flowing around his head," the *Bangor Daily News* reported.

Now others in Duvall's group leapt into the water and tried to free him. One friend "made repeated attempts to keep Duvall's head above the water but Duvall kept slipping out of his grasp," the paper said.

He had been underwater for as much as an hour when rangers finally freed his body from between the rocks. Twenty-five minutes of CPR performed by a paramedic could not save him.

Park Director Buzz Caverly told Doug Kessell of the *Bangor Daily News* that in addition to Duvall, a ranger nearly lost his life in the rescue attempt. "A park ranger involved in the rescue also slipped on some rocks and fell into the white water but was snapped up from the stream by another ranger," Kessell reported. "The ranger was unharmed but a little shaken."

A Misstep or a Rock

Victor J. Pavidis Jr., a thirty-two-year-old man from Revere, Massachusetts, was part of a six-member team climbing Mount Katahdin on February 19, 1980, when he and the partner to whom he was roped, Paul Grossman of Reading, Massachusetts, fell from the icy face of the Chimney. An experienced climber with six years of experience, Pavidis simply met with bad luck—according to the *Bangor Daily News*, he accidentally hanged himself with his climbing rope in the process of a vertical descent. Grossman landed in a snowfield and was not hurt. The other climbers freed Pavidis and tried to revive him, but he did not respond to resuscitation, and they secured him where he was and hiked out for help in bringing him off the mountain.

A climbing party in 1995 met with sheer bad luck on Katahdin on a sunny September day. Bill Mistretta, Rick Baron, and Diane Mailloux made their way up the mountain alongside Michael Lanza and Penny Beach. As Lanza and Mistretta looked for anchors for their belay stances, Mistretta dislodged a rock—one Lanza later described as "two feet by three feet by several inches thick." Baron immediately angled his body to protect Beach and Mailloux, who were below him, but more rocks had begun to fall.

"He was struck by a cantaloupe sized rock above his left eye," the AAC report details. Baron wore a helmet, but the rock knocked it from his head, and the force of the blow threw him backwards about ten feet down the slope. His anchor stopped him, but he was already unconscious from the blow to the head. "He did not regain consciousness and died probably within fifteen minutes," the report said.

"Rock slides are infrequent," Caverly said to writer George Hurley, who completed the AAC report. "This was one of those freak accidents."

This was little comfort to Michael Lanza, who told Hurley, "One of the most frustrating things was that the route we took was well below our ability level." They had taken this route because a ranger at their registration point suggested that they do so, instead of the route they had originally planned. The reason for the ranger's recommendation was not explained in the report, though such suggestions are usually made with safety in mind.

We don't know much about seventy-two-year-old Stanley Sinclair of Aroostook County, whose life ended when he was riding his snowmobile in the area of Nesowadnehunk Lake on January 31, 1985, and collided with another rider. The event went essentially unrecorded by the media, except for a brief mention (and not even by name) in a round-up of fairly recent deaths in the park in a 1998 *Bangor Daily News* story.

Only the tiniest squib in the 1975 archives of the *Portsmouth Herald* noted the passing of twenty-two-year-old Glenn English, who fell from the northern face of Horse Mountain (though the Maine Death Index says Mount Chase) on July 26, 1975. The only fact added by the newspaper was that English was from somewhere in New Hampshire, a fact—the only fact, beyond the date of death—that I was able to verify in the US Social Security Death Index.

Slip, Fall, and Slide on Cathedral Trail

Why is snow on a mountaintop in July so interesting to young people? The novelty of holding a snowball fight in midsummer attracts youngsters and their parents to mountaintops in parks across the country in the summer months, from Mount Rainier, Yosemite, and Yellowstone National Parks out west to Mount Washington, Mount Greylock, and Mount Katahdin in the northeastern states. To sixteen campers and four counselors from Camp Netop in Casco, Maine, in July 1969, the adventure of climbing a mountain in mid-July and encountering winter-like cold toward its peak must have been quite exhilarating, especially for a small group who left Cathedral Trail to get a closer look at a patch of snow.

The entire group of campers and counselors had reached the summit of Katahdin and were on their way down. Accompanied by a junior counselor, three of the boys, including fourteen-year-old Jay Barrett of Oreland, Pennsylvania, spotted the patch of snow and did not realize that it lay in a precarious position on the edge of one of Katahdin's many cliffs. Jay stepped out into the midst of the snow and found that there was nothing beneath it. He plunged over the edge and downward, falling one hundred feet before colliding with the irregular rocks below.

The impact took Jay's life instantly, and he was evacuated by search-and-rescue teams and taken to Eastern Maine General Hospital in Bangor before being returned to his family.

A random incident on the same trail in the summer of 2004 trapped four hikers high up the mountain. On Saturday, June 27, fifty-two-year-old Roger Cooper, visiting from Bangor, and three other people were hiking on Cathedral Trail at about 4,100 feet. Suddenly they saw small rivers of earth moving down around them, and then the rocks above them gave way. Huge boulders, smaller rocks, and flowing dirt rained over them, tumbling down the mountain and partially burying them.

Other hikers, seeing the rockslide from a distance and realizing that there were people in its path, moved as quickly as they could down the trail to find park personnel and report that people were probably trapped in the rubble. The park mobilized immediately, and soon about sixty people, including park staff and volunteer search-and-rescue teams, worked into the night to rescue the hikers. The massive rockslide had trapped Roger Cooper under a five-hundred-pound boulder, abruptly ending his life. Fifty-one-year-old Stacey Hall from Somersworth, New Hampshire, had an injured shoulder but did not need immediate medical treatment, so he was able to walk down the mountain with two other hikers—Will Williams of Wells, Maine, who was fifty-one, and Frank Atkins, also fifty-one, of Huntsville, Alabama—who had been trapped but were unhurt. A helicopter crew removed Cooper's body the following day.

The park closed the Cathedral Trail through July 1 to allow officials to perform a complete inspection to be sure it was safe for hikers. Park director Caverly told the media that the slide "may have been triggered by natural conditions such as the winter's severe frost and heavy spring rain."

Unheeded Warnings

Every park has at least one case of someone losing his or her life by doing something that warning signs, rangers, and common sense make it clear that they should not attempt. In Yellowstone National Park, for example, people leave the boardwalk to walk over the fragile crust surrounding the park's volcano-heated boiling hot springs, fall in (or jump in), and quickly boil to death. In Yosemite National Park, visitors wade out into the middle of a river at the top of a massive waterfall thinking they will get better photos from that angle, until they get carried off by the forceful current and end up washing over the thundering falls. In Glacier National Park, people approach grizzly bears as if they were tame animals in a petting zoo. In several parks in Florida, snorkelers ignore warning signs and proceed into ponds and lakes that contain hungry alligators.

In Baxter State Park, the vast majority of visitors take proper precautions when hiking the park's trails, but one father and son made an especially unfortunate choice. William Rand chose to skid down Marston Slide, a long-closed section of trail on South Brother Mountain, where the granite becomes excessively slippery in spring and summer when it is covered in slick green algae. The algae growth created enough of a hazard that the park closed and rerouted this trail, but this does not stop some hikers looking for an "extreme" experience.

In August 1985, no fewer than three signs warned of the danger on the algae-coated surface, advising hikers to avoid passing there. Some such slides can be a sort of natural thrill ride for visitors, but Marston Slide's steep grade, rocky base, and jagged surroundings make it far too hazardous to try out for the fun of it.

This did not stop Rand and his seven-year-old son, Jason, from laying down life vests on the slippery surface, sitting astride the vests, and shoving themselves down the slimy descent. No one saw exactly what happened next, but the result was a powerful collision with sharp granite boulders.

Caverly and park rangers who came to the site to attempt a rescue were ready to give Rand the benefit of the doubt. Perhaps he had not realized the danger, even though signs emphatically pointed it out. Perhaps he and his young son had merely slipped, as many other hikers had done before they were warned to avoid that particular slope.

In this case, however, the visitor fully intended to do what he did. Other hikers advised the rangers that Rand had told them he planned to ride down Marston Slide.

When rangers arrived on the scene, they found William Rand severely injured, and Jason less injured but needing medical attention. Mercifully, Jason's injuries were not critical, but Rand died on the way to the hospital. William Rand remains the only person ever to sustain fatal injuries on the slide.

"I'm sure they didn't have any knowledge of what could happen if they lost control," Caverly told Jim Emple of the *Bangor Daily News* after the rescue operation brought the Rands off the mountain. He added, "This slide should be totally avoided. The thought of going down it on life jackets is certainly unique."

The Winter of 2017

Ten years had passed since the last time someone had died in Baxter State Park (from a lightning strike in 2007, as described in chapter 3), but the winter of 2017 saw two deaths within a few weeks of each other.

The park has instituted a policy of not releasing the names of the deceased, so the New Hampshire man discovered on February 5 lying dead near the outlet of Abol Pond has remained anonymous. The fifty-six-year-old man had been at Chimney Pond Campground with six friends for two days, and had departed with them on a seventeen-mile skiing trip in the park that morning. When two passing hikers discovered him later in the day, the rest of his party must not have realized he was missing. The New Hampshire man had had what the park's news release called a "medical event." Rangers, a Maine game warden, and the Millinocket Fire Department all arrived at the scene to assist, but their efforts to revive him failed.

The second incident, and the last one to occur since I began writing this book, happened on Mount Katahdin. John H. Stetson, sixty-eight and an East Holden resident, had set out to hike to the summit with his friend Barry Porter and Barry's son, Adam—two of several people with whom Stetson was camped at Daicey Pond Campground. Stetson owned an eponymous engineering firm, Stetson and Watson, as well as a small transport firm.

An avid outdoorsman, Stetson had enjoyed countless outdoor adventures with Porter from the time they were young boys, and the local outdoor community considered him an accomplished climber. Stetson gained a great deal of experience in the wilds of Maine in every season, embracing winter sports as well as warm-weather activities, leading groups into the backcountry, and spending a great deal of time in Baxter State Park. "He'd been there many, many, many times," said Porter to *News Center Maine* the following day. "He used to climb Katahdin with rocks in his backpack to give him a little challenge. He loved the challenge physically and mentally, and he was up for the challenge."

The hikers chose the new Abol Trail, the rerouting of an old trail that the park had closed in 2014 after landslides made it unsafe for hiking. About a mile of the trail now circumnavigates the rockslide area, eliminating some of the former trail's steepness with switchbacks. As the trail approaches the top of the mountain, large boulders create narrow passages and require some scrambling on the way to the conjunction with the old trail. This intersection joins the new trail with Abol Slide, the area where the landslide forced the trail's closing.

Barry Porter turned back after a time, as he was recovering from recent surgery and knew he should not walk as far as he usually would. Adam continued with Stetson up the progressively more challenging trail as they approached Katahdin's table lands, the flatter areas on the way to Baxter Peak. Before reaching this comparatively easy section, however, they came to the precariously icy intersection with Abol Slide extending some 1,000 feet down the mountainside—a corridor of loose boulders, sharp rock slabs, and shelves of solid ice.

Here the hikers encountered an icy patch, nothing new for a hiker of Stetson's caliber, but for some reason, this spot on this day caught him up short. He may have stepped on one of the many wobbly rocks that masquerade as stable footholds—and perhaps one of these rocks tipped, throwing him off balance. Perhaps his reflexes just didn't serve him well at this moment. However it happened, Stetson was standing on the trail one second and falling down Abol Slide the next. He tumbled down the full thousand-foot length of the slide, coming to rest at last at the bottom.

No one could have survived such a fall, not even an outdoorsman like Stetson. Other hikers and climbers leapt from their positions and made haste to alert rangers to the accident, but no amount of rapid action would have made a difference. Stetson was pronounced dead at the scene.

Climbers in the area assisted the rangers and the Wilderness Rescue Team in transporting the man's body off the mountain.

"It shouldn't have been him," Porter told *News Center* reporter Sanaz Tahernia. "He was physically fit, mentally prepared, equipment-wise, knew what he had to have. You would never have expected it would have been him."

EPILOGUE: HOW TO STAY ALIVE
IN BAXTER STATE PARK

I can't emphasize this enough: More than 100,000 people visit Baxter State Park every year, and fewer than one person each year may not live through the experience—and in many years, everyone goes home safely. By following a few simple rules and taking some reasonable precautions, you can make the most of your own visit and come home with lots of photos, videos, and stories to share with your friends and family.

Pay attention to weather reports. Weather on Mount Katahdin and other peaks in the park can change in the course of a few minutes, especially as you make your way higher on the mountain. Sometimes conditions on the mountain are absolutely intolerable for human beings. Don't assume you know what the weather will be like, or that a down parka and crampons will keep you alive. Weather wins. You can hike another day.

Talk to a ranger before your hike or climb. As there are no visitor centers or other facilities in the park, rangers are the best source of information about what conditions may be like on your planned route. Stop at the Baxter State Park headquarters in Millinocket, or find the ranger in your campground (you'll meet him or her when you register to camp). It's also critically important that you tell the ranger where you are going and when you plan to return. If you do get lost or you don't return by your appointed time, this information will tell rangers where to start looking for you.

Sign registries. It's not a quaint custom; it may save your life. Your check-in at the start of your hike will tell people where you intend to go, and your failure to check in at day's end can trigger a search much faster than waiting for your friends or family to realize you haven't come home.

Ask about avalanche danger. If you're climbing or hiking in winter, be aware of your environment and the potential for an avalanche on your route. Here are the conditions that can lead to an avalanche on Katahdin, provided by the Acadia Mountain Guides Climbing School:

- Slopes of 25 to 45 degrees and higher
- Evidence of previous avalanches
- Snow intensity of greater than one inch per hour
- Snow falling in icy (rimed) crystals
- Steady winds moving snow onto leeward slopes
- Rapid temperature changes
- Snowpack temperatures around 32 degrees F (0 degree C) and warming
- Presence of temperature gradients greater than 1 degree/10 cm
- Rain that adds weight to a snowpack
- Persistent cold temperatures that delay bonding and strengthening of the snow
- Accumulation zones in gullies

Watching for these signs still may not reveal an avalanche waiting to happen, however, so talk with rangers to determine the level of danger on the day of your hike, and take their insights to heart.

Don't hike or climb alone. The lure of the wild and the need for solitude may seem very romantic, but in Baxter State Park, several of the hikers and climbers who met a bad end were on their own in an unexpected life-threatening situation. Hiking with one other person or with a group can mean the difference between a terrific day and one that ends in tragedy. At the very least, your companion will know where you are and how to bring others to assist you—so your loved ones won't spend years wondering what became of you in the vastness of the Maine wilderness.

Pack for every possibility. Any time you step out on a trail, you may encounter situations that require an abrupt change of plans. Maybe you miss a turn and find yourself lost in the wilderness. Perhaps a storm front moves in without warning, or someone in your party sustains an injury. Any of these circumstances can extend your time outdoors, turning a day hike into an overnight stay or forcing you to seek cover off-trail.

What should you bring? You're not the first to feel like you might be compromised in the backcountry—in fact, it happens often enough that there's a checklist of things you should have with you every time you hike. The list is known as the Ten Essentials, items that can help you take control of your situation and make it back home in one piece. The list was first developed by the Mountaineers, a club for hikers and climbers back in the 1930s, and they've since updated the list in their book, *Mountaineering: The Freedom of the Hills*, in which they group some individual items to provide a more thorough list. If you carry all of these items with you on every hike, you'll be ready for most of the challenges nature throws at you.

1. Navigation tools: a good map and compass (even if you carry a GPS device)

2. Sun protection: sunscreen and sunglasses

3. Insulation: extra clothing and a poncho

4. Illumination: flashlight and/or headlamp

5. First-aid kit

6. Fire starter: a lighter and/or waterproof matches

7. A repair kit and tools (I add a roll of duct tape to this one.)

8. Nutrition: more food than you think you will need

9. Hydration: more water than you think you will need

10. Emergency shelter: an emergency space blanket or ultralight tarp

Keep in mind that while your smartphone may provide maps and a bright light, there is no cellular service or WiFi in the park's wilderness areas, so don't expect to depend on your phone for directional information. Equally important, it will run out of power in the great outdoors, and you'll have nowhere to charge it (unless you bring a solar charger, but even this won't work if you're stranded overnight). If you're going to bring a GPS device with you, choose one that relies on satellites, not on cellular—and bring extra batteries.

Know your own limits. Not everyone has the skill, strength, or stamina to take on a summit hike, an ice climb up a frozen gully, or a ski run through a narrow chute. Pushing the envelope can be great fun and very satisfying, but it's critical to be realistic about your own ability. If you don't feel like you're ready, put it off for a season and build your skill level instead. At the very least, hike, climb, or ski with someone who has the requisite experience to be sure you get home safely.

Listen to your doctor. Heart attacks and similar medical events are the number one cause of death in Baxter State Park. If your doctor has told you that it's time to stop hiking at higher elevations, take this warning seriously. If you have a medical emergency in the park, your rescue (or the recovery of your body) may require dozens of people and expensive equipment and vehicles to complete—not to mention the emotional cost to your family and friends. Be courteous to those around you and refrain from taking your life in your hands unnecessarily.

Dress properly. When it's seventy degrees and sunny at the base of the mountain, it can be forty degrees and foggy at the top. In winter, a day above freezing at the base can still produce serious, life-threatening cold at the summit. Wear the right clothing, including boots, goggles, gloves, an insulating under layer, and a coat and pants rated for the cold you may encounter.

Above all, be prepared and willing to turn back if the weather changes, if the way is rougher than you expected, or if you realize that your hiking or climbing skills are not up to the task ahead. As visitors to wild places, we love to challenge ourselves and push our bodies to the limit—but our personal safety is our own responsibility.

Please don't become an entry in my next book. Be strong, be daring, but most importantly, be safe.

APPENDIX: LIST OF DEATHS 1933–2017 IN CHRONOLOGICAL ORDER

NAME	AGE	DATE	CAUSE	LOCATION
Leroy Bradeen	51	Oct. 8, 1933	Drowned	Kidney Pond
Sgt. E. R. Barnard	23	June 20, 1944	C-54 plane crash	Fort Mountain
Capt. Roger Inman	42	June 20, 1944	C-54 plane crash	Fort Mountain
First Officer D. N. Gill	29	June 20, 1944	C-54 plane crash	Fort Mountain
Nav. David Reynolds	28	June 20, 1944	C-54 plane crash	Fort Mountain
Flt. Eng. Nordie Byrd	30	June 20, 1944	C-54 plane crash	Fort Mountain
Radio Op Eugene Summer	21	June 20, 1944	C-54 plane crash	Fort Mountain
Purser Sam Berman	28	June 20, 1944	C-54 plane crash	Fort Mountain
Wesley Porter	47	June 3, 1943	Gunshot	Webster Lake T6R10
Alphonse Morency	32	Aug. 8, 1943	Gunshot	Webster Lake T6R10
Ferdinand G. Hunter	45	April 28, 1945	Drowned	First Lake Matagamon
Ethel Pease	18	June 22, 1950	Shot for bear	Kidney Pond Camps
Name unknown		1950s	Heart attack	In car at Foster Field
Admiral Thompson		1953	Heart attack	Fishing at Daicey Pond
George Legassey	34	July 7, 1956	Plane crash	North of Brothers Mtns
Alfred McCafferty	30	July 7, 1956	Plane crash	North of Brothers Mtns
Fred Harrison		1958	Suicide	Cabin at Hudson Pond
Name unknown		1962	Heart attack	Roaring Brook Camp
Margaret Ivusic	52	Oct. 29, 1963	Exposure	Mt. Katahdin
Ranger Ralph Heath	37	Oct. 29, 1963	Exposure	Mt. Katahdin
C. Everett Rayner	65	May 26, 1983	Heart attack	Nesowadnehunk Stream
Roger Hildreth	54	April 1964	Exposure	Basin Ponds T3R9
Robbie Mott	17	July 30, 1965	Exposure	Katahdin Lake Trail

NAME	AGE	DATE	CAUSE	LOCATION
Timothy Mott	3	July 30, 1965	Exposure	Katahdin Lake Trail
Charles Marr		Oct. 1967	Drowned	Trout Brook
Name unknown		Oct. 1967	Drowned	Trout Brook
Name unknown		Oct. 1967	Drowned	Trout Brook
Scott Newlin	27	Aug. 24, 1968	Lightning strike	Chimney Pond Camp
Jay Barrett	14	July 16, 1969	Fall	Second Cathedral
Frank Heath		May 1969	Drowned	South Branch Pond
John Hollis		May 1972	Gunshot	Abol Deadwater
Augustus Aldrich	86	July 8, 1974	Lost	Chimney Pond area
Hollister Kent	56	July 9, 1974	Heart attack	Dry Pond
Thomas Keddy	26	Feb. 1974	Exposure	Below Pamola Peak
Glen English	22	July 26, 1975	Fall	Horse Mountain
Victor J. Pavidis Jr.	33	Feb. 19, 1980	Fall	False Chimney
Charlie Hutton	63	Aug. 2, 1981	Heart attack	Helon Taylor Trail
Welden Boswell	64	Aug. 3, 1981	Heart attack	Katahdin Stream
Steve Hilt	20s	Feb. 8, 1984	Avalanche	Cathedral Trail
Ken Levanway	20s	Feb. 8, 1984	Avalanche	Cathedral Trail
Stanley Sinclair	72	Jan. 31, 1985	Collision	Nesowadnehunk Lake
William T. Rand	36	Aug. 4, 1985	Fall	Marston Slide
Derek C. Quiet	16	Aug. 10, 1986	Fall	Mt. Katahdin Knife Edge
John Brown		June 23, 1986	Heart attack	Nesowadnehunk Stream
David Passalacqua	13	Aug. 27, 1990	Lightning strike	Pamola Peak
Allen M. Jalbert	49	Sept. 13, 1994	Heart attack	Kidney Pond Camps
Adam Frigon	19	Aug. 1, 1994	Asthma attack	Webster Stream
Richard Baron	30	Sept. 2, 1995	Hit by a rock	Pamola Peak
Jeffrey Rubin	53	June 3, 1995	Drowned	Trail to Fort Mountain
Roy A. Owen	77	Aug. 14, 1996	Heart attack	Hunt Trail
Louis McGuinn	32	Dec. 25, 1996	Suicide	Hunt Trail
Philip Duval	38	July 30, 1997	Drowned	Little Niagara Falls
David Graves	47	Aug. 1, 1997	Heart attack	Baxter State Park

NAME	AGE	DATE	CAUSE	LOCATION
Richard Smith Jr.	57	July 27, 1998	Head injury/heart issue	Knife Edge
Samuel Willis II	61	Aug. 31, 1998	Heart attack	Third Cathedral
Dennis Schultz	65	2004	Heart attack	Kidney Pond Camps
Roger Cooper	52	June 27, 2004	Rock slide	Cathedral Trail
Evans Huber	24	Aug. 25, 2007	Lightning strike	Katahdin Stream
Name withheld by park	56	Feb. 5, 2017	Medical event	Abol Pond
John H. Stetson	68	Feb. 18, 2017	Fall	Abol Pond
Name withheld by park	60	July 30, 2017	Medical issue	Chimney Pond Trail

REFERENCES

Introduction

"Baxter State Park SAR Data 1992–2014." Accessed Feb. 28, 2018. SAR-Analysis-Review-1.pdf.

Chow, Jeff. "Appalachian Trail: Mount Katahdin." Backpacker, Sept. 20, 2013, accessed Feb. 28, 2018. https://www.backpacker.com/trips/appalachian-trail-mount-katahdin.

"History." Baxter State Park website, accessed Feb. 28, 2018. https://baxterstatepark.org/shortcodes/history/#/.

Chapter 1

"Ashes to Be Scattered in Forest." *Democrat & Chronicle*, Rochester, NY, Aug. 11, 1965, pp. 11 and 13. Accessed Jan. 18, 2018. https://www.newspapers.com/image/136523158/.

Associated Press. "Mt. Katahdin Area Combed for Two Missing Youths." *Biddeford-Saco Journal*, Biddeford, Maine, Aug. 2, 1965, p. 1. Accessed Jan. 17, 2018. https://www.newspapers.com/image/84056036/.

Claiborne, Bill. "No New Clues Found to Lost Penfield Boys." *Democrat & Chronicle*, Rochester, NY, Aug. 4, 1965, p. 15. Accessed Jan. 17, 2018. https://www.newspapers.com/image/136519930/.

———. "Penfield Brothers' Bodies Found in Maine Woods." *Democrat & Chronicle*, Rochester, NY, Aug. 10, 1965, pp. 1–2A. Accessed Jan. 18, 2018. https://www.newspapers.com/image/136522699/.

———. "Rescue Hopes Lost for Penfield Boys." *Democrat & Chronicle*, Rochester, NY, Aug. 9, 1965, pp. 14–15. Accessed Jan. 18, 2018. https://www.newspapers.com/image/136522453/.

———. "Search for 2 Brothers Awaits Medical Opinion." *Democrat & Chronicle*, Rochester, NY, Aug. 6, 1965, accessed Jan. 18, 2018. https://www.newspapers.com/image/136520668/.

"Maine Woods Combed for 2 Penfield Boys." *Democrat & Chronicle*, Rochester, NY, Aug. 1, 1965, p. 1–2A. Accessed Jan. 17, 2018.

Michaud, Mike. "Brother and Sister of Missing Boys Staying with Grant Family in Hudson." *Nashua Telegraph*, New Hampshire, Aug. 4, 1965, p. 1. Accessed Jan. 17, 2018. https://www.newspapers.com/image/74939341/.

Mott, Greg, personal interview, March 7, 2018.

Mott Reynolds, Martha, and Mike Reynolds, personal interview, March 7, 2018.

Owen, David. *Copies in Seconds: How a Lone Inventor and an Unknown Company Created the Biggest Communication Breakthrough Since Gutenberg.* Simon and Schuster, New York, 2008, p. 204.

"2 Penfield Boys Still Missing in Northern Maine Wilderness." *Democrat & Chronicle*, Rochester, New York, Aug. 2, 1965, p. 1–2A. Accessed Jan. 17, 2018. https://www.newspapers.com/image/136519263/.

United Press International. "Hope Dims for Brothers." *Poughkeepsie Journal*, New York, Aug. 4, 1965, p. 19. Accessed Jan. 17, 2018. https://www.newspapers.com/image/114356381/.

———. "Retarded Youth and Infant Brother Lost in Wilderness." *The Town Talk*, Alexandria, La., Aug. 2, 1965, p. 18. Accessed Jan. 17, 2018. https://www.newspapers.com/image/214711000/.

Wight, Eric. *Life and Death in the North Woods: The Story of the Maine Game Warden Service.* Down East Books, Nov. 7, 2014, pp. 73–75.

Chapter 2

Associated Press. "Girl Mistaken for Bear in Me., Shot Kills Her." *Boston Globe*, June 24, 1950, p. 18.

———. "Girl Shot for Bear, Waitress Mistaken for Animal Prowler Killed By Rifle." *Newport Daily News*, June 23, 1950, p. 3, accessed Feb. 16, 2018. https://www.newspapers.com/image/57022483/?terms=Marshall%2BDoxsee.

———. "Killing Girl for Bear in Maine Costs $700." *The Baltimore Sun*, Sept. 14, 1950, p. 1. Accessed Feb. 16, 2018. https://www.newspapers.com/image/216717623/?terms=Marshall%2BDoxsee.

———. "Thought Girl Was Bear, Slaying Suspect Says." *The Morning News*, Wilmington, Del., July 6, 1950, p. 5. Accessed Feb. 16, 2018. https://www.newspapers.com/image/160665390/?terms=Kidney%2BPond%2BCamps%2Bwaitress%2Bshot.

———. "Waitress, Mistaken for Bear, Slain." *Hattiesburg American*, Miss., June 23, 1950, p. 9. Accessed February 16, 2018. https://www.newspapers.com/image/276950003/?terms=Kidney%2BPond%2BCamps%2Bwaitress%2Bshot.

———. "Warrant Issued in Death of Girl." *The Post-Standard*, Syracuse, NY, July 6, 1950, p. 4. Accessed Feb. 16, 2018. https://www.newspapers.com/image/35948916/?terms=Marshall%2BDoxsee.

"Baxter State Park Fatalities." KatahdinOutdoors.com, accessed Feb. 16, 2018. http://www.katahdinoutdoors.com/bsp/fatalities.html.

"Kidney Pond Camps." KatahdinOutdoors.com, accessed Feb. 16, 2018. http://www.katahdinoutdoors.com/bsp/1940s.html.

"Leroy 'Roy' Bradeen." Findagrave.com, accessed Feb. 16, 2018. https://www.findagrave.com/memorial/70855109.

Record of a Death: Leroy Bradeen, Oct. 8, 1933. Retrieved from Maine Dept. of Health and Human Services, Office of Vital Records, Feb. 19, 2018.

"Rev. and Mrs. West To Be Given Party." *Portland Press Herald*, March 29, 1949, p. 6. Accessed Feb. 16, 2018. https://www.newspapers.com/image/8844000/?terms=Ethel%2BPease.

Sleeper, Frank H. *Baxter State Park and the Allagash River*. Arcadia Publishing, 2002, pp. 43–54.

Spencer, Randy. "A Baxter legacy lives on: Memories of Kidney Pond Camps resonate with former visitors." *Bangor Daily News*, May 29, 2012, accessed Feb. 18, 2018. https://bangordailynews.com/2012/05/29/outdoors/outdoors-extra/a-baxter-legacy-lives-on-memories-of-kidney-pond-camps-resonate-with-former-visitors/.

United States Census, 1940. "Ethel E. Pease, 1940." FamilySearch.org, accessed Feb. 16, 2018. https://www.familysearch.org/search/search/record/results?count=20&query=%2Bgivenname%3AEthel~%20%2Bsurname%3APease~%20%2Bdeath_place%3A%22Millinocket%2C%20ME%22~%20%2Bdeath_year%3A1950-1950~.

"Waterboro." Maine: An Encyclopedia. Accessed Feb. 16, 2018. http://maineanencyclopedia.com/waterboro/?hilite=Bradeen.

Chapter 3

Associated Press. "Lightning in Maine Kills Boy Scout, Burns Friend." *Boston Globe*, Aug. 29, 1990, p. 94. Accessed Jan. 23, 2018. https://secure.pqarchiver.com/boston/doc/294561098.html?FMT=FT&FMTS=ABS:FT&type=current&date=Aug+29%2C+1990&author=Associated+Press&pub=Boston+Globe+%28pre-1997+Fulltext%29&edition=&startpage=84&desc=LIGHTNING+IN+MAINE+KILLS+BOY+SCOUT%2C+BURNS+FRIEND.

———. "Lightning Kills Maine Camper." *Albuquerque Journal*, Aug. 26, 1968, accessed Jan. 29, 2018. https://www.newspapers.com/image/158584011/?terms=Scott%2BNewlin.

———. "Maine Camp Tragedy." *Kane Republican*, Aug. 27, 1968, accessed Jan. 29, 2018. https://www.newspapers.com/image/52385328/?terms=Scott%2BNewlin.

———. "Maine Forest Head Investigates Lightning Death." *The Portsmouth Herald*, NH, Aug. 29, 1968, accessed Jan. 22, 2018. https://www.newspapers.com/image/56495958/?terms=Scott%2BNewlin%2Blightning.

Baxter, Percival Proctor. Mount Katahdin: An Address Given at the Annual Meeting of the Maine Sportsmen's Fish and Game Association, State Capitol, Augusta, Maine, Jan. 27, 1921, p. 10. Accessed Jan. 23, 2018. https://books.google.com/books?id=YKpHAQAAMAAJ&printsec=frontcover&source=gbs_ge_summary_r&cad=0#v=onepage&q&f=false.

REFERENCES

"Ball lightning." Wikipedia, accessed Jan. 21, 2018.

Buckley, Ken. "Lightning Death Investigated." *Bangor Daily News*, Aug. 29, 1968, p. 6.

Clarke, Ronald W. *Benjamin Franklin: A Biography*. Random House, 1983, p. 87, accessed Jan. 21, 2018. https://www.webcitation.org/64dqHa9Zh ?url=http://www.todayinsci.com/R/Richmann_Georg/Richmann GeorgExp.htm.

Dunne, Daisy. "Mystery of ball lightning is finally solved: Eerie orb-like glow is created when radiation gets trapped inside a plasma bubble." DailyMail.com, August 1, 2017, accessed Jan. 21, 2018. http://www. dailymail.co.uk/sciencetech/article-4750304/Ball-lightning-finally -explained-scientists.html#ixzz54rEcpHg3.

Handwerk, Brian. "Ball Lightning: A Shocking Scientific Mystery." *National Geographic News*, May 31, 2006, accessed Jan. 21, 2018. https://news .nationalgeographic.com/news/2006/05/060531-ball-lightning.html.

"How Dangerous is Lightning?" National Weather Service, accessed Jan. 21, 2018. http://www.lightningsafety.noaa.gov/odds.shtml.

Jackson, Charlie, in discussion with the author, Feb. 10, 2018.

Koprowski, Hilary MD. Personal letter to Mr. and Mrs. Caroll C. Newlin, Aug. 29, 1968. Provided by Carol Newlin.

Ley, Willy. "The Great UFO Mystery: Visitors from Outer Space or What?" *The Sunday Herald*, Provo, Utah, Jan. 21, 1968, accessed Jan. 21, 2018. https://www.newspapers.com/image/11866517/?terms=ball%2Blightning %2BMaine.

"Lightning Fatal to Katahdin Camper." *Bangor Daily News*, Aug. 26, 1968, p. 1 and 2.

"Lightning strike kills Maine camper." *Burlington Free Press*, Aug. 27, 2007, p. 2. Accessed Jan. 23, 2018. https://www.newspapers.com/ image/203302175/?terms=Katahdin%2Bdeath.

"Lightning, Maine, Mount Katahdin, Baxter State Park." Accident Reports of the American Alpine Club, 1991. Accessed Jan, 23, 2018. http:// publications.americanalpineclub.org/articles/13199103800/Lightning -Maine-Mount-Katahdin-Baxter-State-Park.

Newlin, Carol M., MD, PhD, in discussion with the author, January 24, 2018.

"Physics Professor Sees Lightning Death as Rare." *Bangor Daily News*, Aug. 27, 1968, p. 3.

Rowe, Joshua Brooking. *The two Widecombe tracts 1638: giving a contemporary account of the great storm*. G.M. for R. Harford, London, 1638, accessed Jan 21, 2018.

"Severe Weather 101." The National Severe Storms Laboratory, accessed Jan. 21, 2018. https://www.nssl.noaa.gov/education/svrwx101/lightning/faq/.

Stenhoff, Mark. "Ball Lightning: An Unsolved Problem in Atmospheric Physics." Springer Science and Business Media, 2006. p. 70.

United Press International. "Philadelphia Camper Killed By Lightning." *Lebanon Daily News*, Penn., Aug. 26, 1968, accessed Jan. 22, 2018. https://www.newspapers.com/image/5434917/?terms=Scott%2BNewlin%2Blightning.

Wilkins, Austin H., and Caverly, Irvin C. "Scott Newlin Tragedy, Baxter State Park Authority, Augusta, Maine." State of Maine, Baxter State Park Authority, Sept. 24, 1968.

Woog, Adam. *Zombies*. ReferencePoint Press, San Diego, Calif., 2011, p. 43. Accessed Jan. 21, 2018.

Wu, H.-C. "Relativistic-microwave theory of ball lightning." *Scientific Reports*, Vol. 6, June 22, 2016, doi:10.1038/srep28263. https://www.nature.com/articles/srep28263.

"Your Odds of Getting Zika." Casino.org, accessed Jan. 22, 2018. https://www.casino.org/zika-odds/.

Chapter 4

Associated Press. "Body of Ranger Found on Maine Mountain Peak." *Hartford Courant*, May 18, 1964, p. 36, accessed Jan. 24, 2018. https://www.newspapers.com/image/237668906/?terms=Ralph%2BHeath.

———. "Body of Rescue Ranger Found." *Nashua Telegraph*, NH, May 19, 1964, p. 5. Accessed Jan. 24, 2018. https://www.newspapers.com/image/74922664/?terms=Ralph%2BHeath.

———. "Body of Woman Hiker is Found." *The Baltimore Sun*, Apr. 30, 1964, p. 9, accessed Jan. 24, 2018. https://www.newspapers.com/image/219112082/?terms=Katahdin.

———. "End Search of Katahdin for Hildreth." *Boston Globe*, May 14, 1964, p. 9.

———. "Mountain Team Renews Search." *Portsmouth Herald*, NH, May 16, 1964, p. 19. Accessed Jan. 24, 2018. https://www.newspapers.com/image/56549409/?terms=Ralph%2BHeath.

———. "Rescue Team Begins Search." *Biddeford-Saco Journal*, Apr. 29, 1964, p. 1, accessed Jan. 24, 2018. https://www.newspapers.com/image/86110450/?terms=Katahdin.

Austin, Phyllis. *Wilderness Partners: Buzz Caverly and Baxter State Park*. Op. cit., pp. 94-97.

Baxter State Park Authority. "Report of Proceedings: Mt. Katahdin Tragedy Board of Review/Conducted Jointly by Baxter State Park Authority and Maine Department of Inland Fisheries and Game." 1964, accessed Jan. 23, 2018. http://digitalmaine.com/cgi/viewcontent.cgi?article=1001&context=baxter_park_docs.

Dunn, Gordon E., and staff. "The Hurricane Season of 1963." *Monthly Weather Review*, Vol. 92, No. 3, March 1964, pp. 128-142. Accessed Jan. 23, 2018. http://www.aoml.noaa.gov/general/lib/lib1/nhclib/mwreviews/1963.pdf.

"Exonerate Plourde in Hildreth Case." *Boston Globe*, May 22, 1964, p. 11.

"Hildreth's Body Found on Katahdin." *Boston Globe*, June 1, 1965, p. 3.

Kick, Peter W. *Desperate Steps: Life, Death, and Choices Made in the Mountains of the Northeast*. Appalachian Mountain Club Books, Boston, Mass., 2015, p. 10–11.

"Lowell Man Agrees to Submit to Lie Detector at Portland." *Boston Globe*, May 21, 1964, p. 29.

"No Foul Play Seen in Me. Death." *Boston Globe*, June 2, 1965, p. 8.

"No Trace in Five Days Of Man Lost on Katahdin." *Boston Globe*, May 13, 1964, p. 4.

Putnam, William L. "Maine, Mt. Katahdin." AAJ Accidents, American Alpine Club, 1964, accessed Jan. 24, 2018. http://publications.americanalpine club.org/articles/13196402901/Maine-Mt-Katahdin.

"Slaying on Mt. Katahdin?" *Boston Globe*, May 18, 1964, p. 12.

Sullivan, Jerome. "A Lowell Man Vanishes . . . and Mt. Katahdin Mystery Grows." *Boston Globe*, May 24, 1964, p. 14.

United Press International. "Maine Cop Joins Climber Hunt." *The Bridgeport Post*, Conn., May 12, 1964, accessed Jan. 29, 2018. https://www.news papers.com/image/60251320/?terms=Ralph%2BHeath.

Wight, Eric. *Life and Death in the North Woods: The Story of the Maine Game Warden Service*. Down East Books, Nov. 7, 2014, pp. 86–88.

Chapter 5

"Alfred S. McCafferty." Findagrave.com, accessed March 11, 2018. https://www.findagrave.com/memorial/78644409/alfred-s.-mccafferty.

Arsenault, Mark, and DePaul, Tony. "Mountainside Monument." *Boston Globe*, June 1, 2009, p. B1, accessed Jan. 30, 2018. http://pqasb.pqarchiver.com/boston/doc/405173815.html?FMT=FT&FMTS=ABS:FT&type=current&date=Jun+1%2C+2009&author=Arsenault%2C+Mark%7C%7C%7C%7C%7C%7CDePaul%2C+Tony&pub=Boston+Globe&edition=&startpage=B.1&desc=Mountainside+monument.

Associated Press. "Swarm of Planes Scour Woods for Pair Lost in Me." *Daily Boston Globe*, July 16, 1956, p. 13.

Buckley, Ken. "Wreckage Found at Sourdnahunk." *Bangor Daily News*, Me., May 15, 1968, p.1 and 4.

"Continuing Hunt for Missing Maine Plane." *Lewiston Evening Journal*, Me., July 13, 1956, accessed Feb. 17, 2018 at Findagrave.com. https://www.findagrave.com/memorial/151115124.

"Editor's Desk." TARPA Topics: The Active Retired Pilots Association of TWA, January 1988, p. 17. Accessed Jan. 30, 2018. https://issuu.com/tarpa_topics/docs/1988.02.tarpa_topics.

Noddin, Peter. "C-54A 'Skymaster' 41-37227, 20 June 1944, Fort Mountain, Near Millinocket, North Atlantic Wing Air Transport Command."

Maine Wreck Chasers, accessed Jan. 30, 2018. http://www.mewreck chasers.com/C54A.html.

———. "List-9.docx: List of Military Aircraft Accidents in Maine," accessed Jan. 30, 2018. http://www.mewreckchasers.com.

"Plane Overdue at Millinocket." *Lewiston Daily Sun*, Me., July 11, 1956, accessed Feb. 17, 2018 at Findagrave.com. https://www.findagrave.com/memorial/151115124.

Radecki, Alan. "Tales from the Flying Circus, Part Deux." Vintage Air blog, March 12, 2013, accessed Jan. 30, 2018. http://vintageairphotos.blogspot.com/2013/03/tales-from-flying-circus-part-deux.html.

Sambides, Nick. "Baxter State Park discourages visits to crash site." *Bangor Daily News*, June 25, 2009, accessed Jan. 30, 2018. https://bangordailynews.com/2009/06/25/news/baxter-state-park-discourages-visits-to-crash-site/.

"Schools." *Flying Magazine*, January 1930, p. 46. Accessed Jan. 30, 2018.

Sneddon, Rob. "The Wreck Chaser." *Down East*, accessed Jan. 30, 2018. https://downeast.com/the-wreck-chaser/.

War Department, US Army Air Force. "Accident No. 44-6-210-67, Report of Aircraft Accident." Official record including memoranda, official reports, telegrams, wire reports, and certificates of death diagnoses. June 21–July 12, 1944.

Chapter 6

Associated Press. "Bloodhound Brought to Maine to Track Slayer." *Boston Globe*, Aug. 7, 1943, p. 1.

———. "Hold Funeral for Slain Patten Guide." *Lewiston Daily Sun*, June 10, 1943, accessed Feb. 17, 2018. https://wesleyporter.weebly.com/murder.html.

———. "Patten Guide Slain, Dr. Pritham Reports." *Lewiston Sun-Journal*, June 5, 1943, accessed Feb. 17, 2018. https://wesleyporter.weebly.com/murder.html.

———. "Slain Guide's Body Brought to Augusta." *Lewiston Sun-Journal*, July 15, 1943, accessed Feb. 17, 2018. https://wesleyporter.weebly.com/murder.html.

"The Great North Woods Mystery." *True Detective*, February 1944, Vol. 41, No. 5.

"Hermit Is Shot Fatally in Maine Murder Manhunt." *Boston Globe*, Aug. 9, 1943, p. 16.

Nickerson, Mark. "Real Life Stories of a Maine State Trooper: Maine's then-biggest manhunt." Wesley Porter Tribute website, Sept. 15, 2009, accessed Feb. 17, 2018. https://wesleyporter.weebly.com/murder.html.

———. "The Manhunt." Wesley Porter Tribute website, Sept. 15, 2009, accessed Feb. 18, 2018. https://wesleyporter.weebly.com/manhunt.html.

"No Arrest Yet in Fatal Shooting at Webster Lake." *Bangor Daily News*, June 5, 1943, p. 1 and 15.

"No Solution Yet of Webster Lake Slaying." *Bangor Daily News*, June 7, 1943, p. 1.

Ricker, Nok-Noi. "Manhunt for Parkman murderer one of longest in Maine history." *Bangor Daily News*, Oct. 3, 2017, accessed Feb. 18, 2018. https://bangordailynews.com/2015/08/09/news/state/manhunt-for-parkman-murder-suspect-one-of-longest-in-maine-history/.

"Wesley Porter, Maine Guide, Patten, Me." Accessed Feb. 18, 2018. https://wesleyporter.weebly.com.

Wight, Eric. *Life and Death in the North Woods: The Story of the Maine Game Warden Service.* Down East Books, Nov. 7, 2014, pp. 69–73. Accessed Feb.18, 2018.

"Woodsman Sought in Porter Slaying Fatally Shot By Posse." *Bangor Daily News*, Aug. 9, 1943, p. 1.

Chapter 7

Allen, Mel. "Making the Final Choice on Katahdin." *Yankee Magazine*, February 1980, reprinted in New England Today Aug. 13, 2008, accessed Feb. 20, 2018. https://newengland.com/today/living/new-england-history/mt-katahdin-survival/.

Associated Press. "Body Recovered on Me. Mountain." *Nashua Telegraph*, NH, Feb. 7, 1974, accessed Feb. 20, 2018. https://www.newspapers.com/image/78279287/?terms=Thomas%2BKeddy.

Hamilton, George. "Exposure, Frostbite, Exceeding Abilities—Maine Mt. Katahdin." American Alpine Club, 1974, accessed Feb. 19, 2018. http://publications.americanalpineclub.org/articles/13197501100/print.

Howe, Nicholas. "Two-Track Triple Threat." *Skiing*, spring 1984, accessed Feb. 20, 2018.

United Press International. "Climber Lost on Mt. Katahdin." *Naugatuck Daily News*, Conn., Feb. 5, 1974, accessed Feb. 19, 2018. https://www.newspapers.com/image/75087622/?terms=Thomas%2BKeddy.

———. "Stranded Climber Dies at State Park in Maine." *Hartford Courant*, Conn., Feb. 3, 1974, accessed Feb. 20, 2018. https://www.newspapers.com/image/237083462/?terms=Thomas%2BKeddy.

Chapter 8

Borden, Tom. "Augustus vs. Terrible Mountain." *Vermont Life*, summer 1974, vol. 28, no. 4, pp. 26-28.

"Building the World: The Founding of Brasilia, Brazil." University of Massachusetts at Boston, accessed Feb. 21, 2018. https://www.newspapers.com/image/200392815/?terms=Hollister%2BKent.

REFERENCES

"Hollister Kent (obituary)." *Bennington Banner*, Vt. July 12, 1974, p. 14. Accessed Feb. 21, 2018. https://www.newspapers.com/image/63037502/?terms=Augustus%2BAldrich.

Palm, Kathleen. "Majestic Mt. Katahdin looms as nature's beckoner and killer." *Bennington Banner*, July 16, 1974, p. 3. Accessed Feb. 21, 2018. https://www.newspapers.com/image/63038346/.

"Search ends for hiker on Katahdin." *Bangor Daily News*, July 12, 1974, accessed Feb. 21, 2018. https://news.google.com/newspapers?nid=2457&dat=19740712&id=A-kzAAAAIBAJ&sjid=CzkHAAAAIBAJ&pg=2290,4295587&hl=en.

United Press International. "Planner Hollister Kent dies on search for Katahdin hiker." *Bennington Banner*, July 10, 1974, p. 18, accessed Feb. 21, 2018. https://www.newspapers.com/image/63037055/?terms=Augustus%2BAldrich.

———. "Search pressed for Vermont hiker, age 86, on Katahdin." *Bennington Banner*, July 8, 1974, p. 14. Accessed Feb. 21, 2018. https://www.newspapers.com/image/63036634/?terms=Augustus%2BAldrich.

"Weather history results for Millinocket, Me., July 5, 1974." *Farmer's Almanac*, accessed Feb. 21, 2018, https://www.farmersalmanac.com/weather-history/search-results/.

Wight, Eric. *Life and Death in the North Woods: The Story of the Maine Game Warden Service*. Down East Books, Nov. 7, 2014, pp. 76–77.

Chapter 9

Associated Press. "2 From Upstate Killed on Climb as Snow Slides." *New York Times*, Feb. 8, 1984, accessed Feb. 22, 2018. http://www.nytimes.com/1984/02/09/nyregion/2-from-upstate-killed-on-climb-as-snow-slides.html.

———. "Avalanche Danger Closes Katahdin Route." *Boston Globe*, Feb. 12, 1984, p. 1.

Caverly, Irvin. "Avalanche, Weather—Maine, Baxter State Park, Mount Katahdin." American Alpine Club Accident Reports, 1985. Accessed Feb. 22, 2018. http://publications.americanalpineclub.org/articles/13198505302/Avalanche-Weather-Maine-Baxter-State-Park-Mount-Katahdin.

Jackson, Peter. "Climber saves 2 after avalanche, but 2 die." *Press and Sun-Bulletin*, Binghamton, NY, Feb. 9, 1984, p. 2, accessed Feb. 22, 2018. https://www.newspapers.com/image/256181061/?terms=Ken%2BLevanway%2BTroy%2BNY.

"Maine Avalanche Kills 2 Climbers." *Poughkeepsie Journal*, Feb. 9, 1984, p. 3., accessed Feb. 22, 2018. https://www.newspapers.com/image/114586307/.

Olson, Wyatt. "Hiker's fall points up winter rules." *Bangor Daily News*, Jan. 29, 1998, B1 and B6. Accessed Feb. 22, 2018. https://news.google.com/

newspapers?nid=2457&dat=19980129&id=GAtbAAAAIBAJ&sjid=J04
NAAAAIBAJ&pg=1421,3446508.

United Press International. "Two hikers buried under an avalanche of heavy,
wet snow." UPI Archives, Feb. 9, 1984, accessed Feb. 22, 2018. https://
www.upi.com/Archives/1984/02/09/Two-hikers-buried-under-an
-avalanche-of-heavy-wet/4035445150800/.

Chapter 10

Associated Press. "Weather Prevents Recovery of Body." *Boston Globe*, Aug. 12,
1986, p. 22.

Lagasse, Mary Anne. "Hiker falls to death on Mount Katahdin." *Bangor Daily
News*, Aug. 11, 1986, pp. 1 and 2.

———. "Rain, fatigue postpone removal of hiker's body." *Bangor Daily News*,
Aug. 12, 1986, p. 1.

———. "Hiker's body recovered on Katahdin." *Bangor Daily News*, Aug. 13,
1986, p. 8.

Tetreault, Steve. "Trail's End." The Bear Dogs of Katahdin (and Other Recollections of a Baxter Park Ranger) Facebook page, Aug. 8, 2017, repost
from Oct. 8, 2015, accessed Feb. 26, 2018. https://www.facebook.com/
TheBearDogsofKatahdin/.

———. *The Bear Dogs of Katahdin (and Other Recollections of a Baxter Park
Ranger)*. Chapter 5: The Mountain Has Secrets. Xlibris, 2007.

———. Personal conversation by telephone, Feb. 2, 2018.

Chapter 11

Associated Press. "Climber dies scaling 100th peak." *Newark Advocate*, Ohio,
June 7, 1995, p. 8. Accessed Feb. 27, 2018. https://www.newspapers.com/
image/289379759/?terms=Jeffrey%2BRubin.

———. "Climbing prof dies on last of 100 peaks." *The Lincoln Star*, Nebraska,
June 6, 1995, p. 1, accessed Feb. 27, 2018. https://www.newspapers.com/
image/311872549/?terms=Jeffrey%2BRubin.

Imhoff, Ernest F. "The seductive, occasionally fatal allure of peak bagging." *Baltimore Sun*, June 25, 1995, p. 61 and 66, accessed Feb. 27, 2018. https://
www.newspapers.com/image/373620549/.

"Jeffrey Rubin, negotiation expert, Tufts professor, and hiker; at 53." *Boston
Globe* obituaries, June 7, 1995, p. 35.

Menkel-Meadow, Carrie. "Introduction: What Will We Do When Adjudica-
tion Ends? A Brief Intellectual History of ADR." Georgetown University Law Center, UCLA Law Review 1613 (1997), p. 1626 (PDF p. 15).
Accessed Feb. 27, 2018. https://scholarship.law.georgetown.edu/cgi/
viewcontent.cgi?referer=https://www.google.com/&httpsredir=1&article
=2773&context=facpub.

Saxon, Wolfgang. "Jeffrey Z. Rubin, 54, an Expert on Negotiation." *The New York Times*, June 9, 1995, accessed Feb. 27, 2018. http://www.nytimes .com/1995/06/09/obituaries/jeffrey-z-rubin-54-an-expert-on -negotiation.html.

"250 attend memorial service." *The News-Press*, Fort Myers, Fla., June 8, 1995, p. 8. Accessed Feb. 27, 2018. https://www.newspapers.com/image/ 216804728/?terms=Jeffrey%2BRubin.

Walsh, Pamela M. "Tufts professor dies on peak." *Boston Globe*, June 5, 1995, p. 13.

Chapter 12

Associated Press. "Boy Killed on Mt. Katahdin." July 17, 1969, p. 2, accessed Feb. 26, 2018. https://www.newspapers.com/image/56452468/?terms =Second%2BCathedral%2BKatahdin.

———. "Katahdin's Cathedral Trail Closed Until July 1 Following Fatal Rock Slide." *World and US Highpoints News*, June 28, 2004, accessed Feb. 27, 2018. http://www.network54.com/Forum/3897/message/1088428633/ Katahdin%27s+Cathedral+Trail+Closed+Until+July+1+Following+ Fatal+Rock+Slide.

———. "Oreland Boy Killed in Fall on Mountain." *The Morning Call*, Allentown, Penn., July 18. 1969, p. 11, accessed Feb. 26, 2018. https://www .newspapers.com/image/281561080/?terms=Jay%2BBarrett%2B Katahdin.

"Bay State Man Falls to Death." *Burlington Free Press*, Feb. 22, 1980, p. 18, accessed Feb. 22, 2018. https://www.newspapers.com/image/199319657/ ?terms=Victor%2BJ.%2BPavidis.

Emple, Jim. "Man is killed from slide in Baxter Park." *Bangor Daily News*, Aug. 6, 1985, p. 15.

Gagnon, Dawn, and Judy Harrison. "Climber, 68, dies in 1,000 foot fall in Baxter State Park." *Bangor Daily News*, Feb. 20, 2017, accessed Feb. 27, 2018. http://bangordailynews.com/2017/02/20/news/state/climber-68 -dies-in-1000-foot-fall-in-baxter-state-park/.

"Granite Stater Killed Climbing." *Portsmouth Herald*, July 28, 1975, accessed Feb. 21, 2018. https://newspaperarchive.com/portsmouth-herald-jul-28 -1975-p-1/.

Green, Bill. "Accomplished climber who fell to his death on Katahdin identified." News Center Maine, Feb. 21, 2017, accessed Feb. 27, 2018. http:// www.newscentermaine.com/article/news/local/accomplished-climber -who-fell-to-his-death-on-katahdin-identified/410249680.

"Houlton Man is Drowned at Matagamon Lake." *Bangor Daily News*, April 30, 1945, p. 1 and 3.

Hurley, George, and Michael Lanza. "Falling Rock, Poor Position, Maine, Mount Katahdin, Chimney Pond." American Alpine Club Accident

Report, 1996, accessed Feb. 22, 2018. http://publications.americanalpine club.org/articles/13199605102/Falling-Rock-Poor-Position-Maine -Mount-Katahdin-Chimney-Pond.

Kessell, Doug. "Virginia man dies in Baxter stream." *Bangor Daily News*, July 31, 1997, p. 8.

"Montco Boy, 14, Dies in Cliff Fall." *Philadelphia Daily News*, July 17, 1969, p. 4, accessed Feb. 26, 2018. https://www.newspapers.com/image/ 184972874/?terms=Jay%2BBarrett%2BKatahdin.

"News in Brief: Climber's Body is Recovered." *Boston Globe*, Feb. 22, 1980, p. 1.

Olson, Wyatt. "Hiker's fall points up winter rules." *Bangor Daily News*, Jan. 29, 1998, B1 and B6. Accessed Feb. 22, 2018. https://news.google.com/ newspapers?nid=2457&dat=19980129&id=GAtbAAAAIBAJ&sjid= J04NAAAAIBAJ&pg=1421,3446508.

"Rock slide kills hiker in Maine." *Burlington Free Press*, June 28, 2004, p. 2, accessed Feb. 27, 2018. https://www.newspapers.com/image/ 203311323/?terms=Katahdin%2Bdeath.

Sambides Jr., Nick. "Skier dies in Baxter State Park after getting separated from group." *Bangor Daily News*, Feb. 6, 2017, accessed Feb. 27, 2018. http://bangordailynews.com/2017/02/06/outdoors/n-h-skier-dies-in-baxter-state-park-after-getting-separated-from-his-group/.

Tahernia, Sanaz. "Hiker that died in Baxter State Park remembered." News Center Maine, Feb. 21, 2017, accessed Feb. 27, 2018. http://www .newscentermaine.com/article/news/local/katahdin/hiker-that-died-in -baxter-state-park-remembered/411067446.

INDEX

ABOUT THE AUTHOR

Randi Minetor has written more than thirty books for Globe Pequot and Lyons Press, including *Historic Glacier National Park*, *Death in Glacier National Park*, *Death in Zion National Park*, and *Death on Mount Washington*. She lives in Rochester, New York.